Unlocking the Mystery

An Introduction to God Manifestation

Community Edition

Jason Hensley

Speaking of His Glory
A Christadelphian Publication
Jason@speakingofhisglory.com
Copyright November 2009

INTRODUCTION

This book has been written for those who are looking for answers. If the Trinity has ever been confusing to you, if the relationship between Jesus and his Father, as taught by the churches is something that doesn't make sense, or that has frustrated you before, this book was written for you. It is a book that strives to look deeply into the Trinity, to unveil the contradictions that it brings about, and to search through the Scriptures and see what the Word of God truly teaches. In doing so, we will be led to the concept of God manifestation.

God manifestation is a topic which is of key importance for the people of God. It envelops our understanding of who God is, it pertains to our relationship with Jesus, it helps us to more firmly grasp the hope of the Kingdom, and it shows us how we should be living our lives in the here and now. This book has been written as an introduction to the subject, as something that will whet your excitement and fan the flames of your zeal for the Truth.

Over the past four years, this subject has captured my love and my enthusiasm. All of us will find a study in it to be beneficial. In no way is this study meant to be exhaustive, but an introduction to the subject; it is my hope that it will stimulate your interest in personal Bible study. The world will continue to grow and develop in its knowledge of all of the things that it deems important, and so may the people of God continue to grow in knowledge of His Word. As you read through this book, may that desire and fire for an understanding of Scripture burn within you, for this is truly the attitude that the Father seeks in His children. As the Apostle wrote:

"Prove all things; hold fast to that which is good."
1 Thessalonians 5:21

We are called to have an attitude that burns for the Truth. We are to seek for it, to grab on to it and never let it go. The Christadelphians are a group of Bible students that seek to do exactly that. They are not perfect, but they strive to understand God's Truth in SINCERITY and apply it in LOVE. It has been a gift to have them in my life. If this book helps to answer your questions and reveal the Truth about God, seek out the Christadelphians and learn more about them. You can find out about them and connect to them on ThisIsYourBible.com.

As you embark on this journey through God manifestation, my prayer for you is that God will use these words to draw you nearer to Him, and that this book will help resolve some of the unanswered questions you may have had about the Creator of this universe.

The worksheets that are at the end of every chapter are meant to help you retain more of the material from the chapter. I think you will enjoy them. Any feedback is appreciated. jason@speakingofhisglory.com

In the hope of Zion's King,
THE AUTHOR

TABLE OF CONTENTS

UNLOCKING THE MYSTERY

CHAPTER 1

THE MYSTERY OF GOD

"Exactly, it doesn't make sense. It's not going to. No one can understand how a son can be the same as his Father. That's because the Trinity is a mystery, and we will never be able to understand God completely. Don't even try. He is holy and sacred. If you could actually understand Him, He wouldn't truly be God."

This may be a familiar scene. Often when we are talking to people about in the Trinity, we may end up saying "I don't understand! What you are telling me does not make any sense at all. A son cannot be his own Father;" or, "Yes, but no one has ever seen God, and yet you are telling me that Jesus is God. Many people saw Jesus." Often the reply is in the form of, "That's right. Your question is true, but the Trinity does not make sense. It isn't supposed to. You won't be able to understand it because it is referring to the Ruler of the universe. It is a great mystery." Here are some Christian testimonies that voice this idea:

"The Father is God; the Son is God; and the Holy Ghost is God. Yet the Father, the Son, and the Holy Ghost, are not three gods, but ONE GOD. This is a <u>MIGHTY MYSTERY</u>." *The Mighty Mystery*; George W. Mylne; Pgs. 8-9

1

"That there are three persons in one God is <u>a mystery</u> which human reason, left to its own resources, can neither discover nor demonstrate." *The Divine Trinity*; Joseph Pohle; Pg. 194

"I believe in the supreme Deity of the Father, Son, and Holy Ghost. I believe that these are in one respect *three*, and in another respect *one*. I believe these facts, because they are revealed in the Sacred Volume. But how they are three, and yet but one, is <u>a mystery</u>." *Works of the Late Reverend John Paul*; John Paul and Stewart Bates; Pg. 113

Mystery is a word that often comes up when we are seeking answers to the Trinity. It is the way in which people are told not to dig any deeper, not to search further, not to really push for Truth. It is a word that is used to turn people in a different direction, to cover up the fact that there really is no answer to their question. Instead of ministers and pastors searching through the Scriptures to try to make sense of apparent contradictions, they lightly dismiss the contradictions as a mystery that they cannot find out, and those church-members who do not search any further are deemed "faithful" because they do not seek for answers to their questions.

This is not the case. There are answers to the contradictions in the Trinity, and through this study, we will seek to make sense of the questions, "How can Jesus be God and the son of God at the same time?" and "How could a son be the same being as his Father?" The doctrine of the Trinity can tend to bring these types of questions to our minds. And thankfully, there are answers. The Bible is a book written to us, in order to help us understand God's purpose for the earth, and also to help us understand God! Some people may say that "there are many mysteries in the Word, and if you could understand God, then He wouldn't really be God." But, while this is true—we will not understand the very intricacies of God—we can still learn and understand what He has told us in His Word. In this book on God Manifestation, we have four overall goals:

1. *To get to know and understand God more deeply.*
2. *To learn about the relationship between Him and Jesus.*
3. *To see if what we have learned applies to us and to our lives.*
4. *To see that Scripture makes sense!*

We will fulfill these goals in this first chapter by delving into the word "mystery" and exploring its use in Scripture. The point of this, and basically the point of this chapter, will be to show us that it really does matter what we believe about God, and to demonstrate that we HAVE to search through the Scriptures to understand the Truth about Him. We will show that we have to urgently search out and understand the relationship between Christ and his Father. To finish the chapter, we will spend time actually trying to understand our Father and who He is. We will talk about His structural aspects, His purpose, and His character. As we strive to meet these four goals in the next chapter, we will see how the Father's character and name go together, and spend time examining the term "God Manifestation." In chapter 3, we will spend a few pages looking at the angels and their relation to God's name. The fourth chapter will take what we learned in the previous chapters and apply it to Christ. In the following chapter we will see how this concept actually envelops and embraces our own personal hope. The sixth chapter will then try to look at one of the passages that people show to us when they are trying to explain the Trinity, and show that the passage actually doesn't teach what many believe it to teach. Finally, in the last chapter before the conclusion, we will explore the atonement and recognize that the death and resurrection of Christ was all about exalting the Father and leading us to God manifestation. May these studies serve to reinforce and strengthen our faith, so that we can be found ready when the master returns.

THE REVEALED MYSTERY

In Matthew 13, we see the first instance of the word "mystery" (actually translated as "mysteries" in Matthew, but the word is the same in the Greek) in the Bible. Scripture goes on to use this Greek word an additional 26 times. As we look into this word and how it is used, a few things will really stand out to us. Let's take a look and see what we can find.

> And the disciples came, and said unto him, Why speakest thou unto them in parables? He answered and said unto them, Because it is given unto you <u>to know the mysteries of the kingdom of heaven</u>, but to them it is not given. For whosoever hath, to him shall be given, and he shall have more abundance: but whosoever hath not, from him shall be taken away even that he hath. Therefore speak I to them in parables: because they seeing see not; and hearing they hear not, neither do they understand. And in them is fulfilled the prophecy of Esaias, which saith, By hearing ye shall hear, and shall not understand; and seeing ye shall see, and shall not perceive: for this people's heart is waxed gross, and their ears are dull of hearing, and their eyes they have closed; lest at any time they should see with their eyes, and hear with their ears, and should understand with their heart

and should be converted, and I should heal them. Matthew 13:10-15

Look at how mystery is used here! This was something that was known to the disciples, that Jesus had actually revealed to them. They KNEW the mysteries of the kingdom of heaven! It wasn't a secret to them, it wasn't something hidden or something that was undiscoverable to them. This is a common characteristic of the word "mystery." Take a look at four more examples. Every time we are told about a mystery in the Bible, we are told that it is something that has been revealed to the faithful, or is understandable to them.

"Wherein he hath abounded toward us in all wisdom and prudence; having made known unto us the mystery of his will, according to his good pleasure which he hath purposed in himself." Ephesians 1:8-9

"Even the mystery which hath been hid from ages and from generations, but now is made manifest to his saints: to whom God would make known what is the riches of the glory of this mystery among the Gentiles; which is Christ in you, the hope of glory." Colossians 1:26-27

"Write the things which thou hast seen, and the things which are, and the things which shall be hereafter; the mystery of the seven stars which thou sawest in my right hand, and the seven golden candlesticks. The seven stars are the angels of the seven churches: and the seven candlesticks which thou sawest are the seven churches." Revelation 1:19-20

"And the angel said unto me, wherefore didst thou marvel? I will tell thee the mystery of the woman, and of the beast that

carrieth her, which hath the seven heads and ten horns."
Revelation 17:7

All of the above are instances of the word "mystery" being used as something that is hidden to the world but not to the saints! Note that in your mind. As we were told in Matthew 13, it was given to the disciples <u>to know</u> the mysteries of the kingdom of God. In fact, this point is solidified when one looks at all 27 instances in which the word "mystery" is used. Every single one of those times tell us that the mystery is in some way understandable! When the Bible uses the word "mystery," it isn't referring to something that we will never understand! The mystery has been revealed to the true believers! "Mystery" isn't a wall that we can hide behind when we don't want to search out God's Testimony for ourselves. Jesus is very straightforward: all those who have will be given more, but whoever does not have will lose even what he has. Those who don't have the desire to learn will never find out, and the understanding that would have been given to them will be given to those who actively search.

This is a weighty message that we must understand. Jesus said that he spoke in parables for the specific purpose of confusing people, so that those who heard him would have to think. They could just listen to him and think "Wow, that was a nice story about planting seeds." Or, they could say, "Wait a minute. This story had a little more to it than I understood." And they could come to Jesus to try to understand. Those were the people who would understand the mysteries of the Kingdom. The Kingdom would always stay a secret to those people who thought that his parables were just nice stories because they would never look deeper into his words. It would be a mystery to them. They would never know the Truth.

The disciples were different. The mystery had been revealed to them because they were willing to come up to Jesus and ask what the parables meant, they were willing to search for an answer. They could hear because their hearts were willing to understand. Their minds were open and they longed to know the Truth. Hence, we see them coming to Jesus and asking what his parables were about in verse 36. But, as Jesus goes on to say, the multitudes were different. They were fulfilling the prophecy of Isaiah chapter 6, which said that "By hearing ye shall hear and not understand: and seeing ye shall see, and shall not perceive." It said that the people had all of the physical faculties, yet they were blind and deaf. Why? Because their hearts had "grown dull" (see the English Standard Version); they had lazy and uncaring hearts. In addition, their ears were dull, and THEY had closed their eyes. They didn't want to know, and the words of Christ were not important to them. They did not have the searching heart that cried out for understanding—the mystery would never be revealed to them.

In looking back through Scripture, we can actually see that this apathetic attitude toward God's word is a characteristic of the Jews. In fact, their lack of knowledge and understanding, rather, their refusal to search out and accept the Truth, is the reason that so many things befell them all throughout the Bible. God had given them the law, He had given them hundreds of prophecies through which they could understand His plan and learn to live how He desired, and yet they disregarded His message, and instead clung to their traditions.

"My people are destroyed for lack of knowledge: because thou hast rejected knowledge, I will also reject thee, that thou shalt be no priest to me: seeing thou hast forgotten the law of thy God, I will also forget thy children." Hosea 4:6

Israel had no knowledge! They forgot about the law, they never learned the lessons that it was supposed to teach them! They didn't truly know their God. We can see this lack of knowledge leading to disastrous effects in their crucifixion of Jesus. They didn't know that they were crucifying their Messiah, their savior sent from God.

"But ye denied the Holy One and the Just, and desired a murderer to be granted unto you; and killed the Prince of life, whom God hath raised from the dead; whereof we are witnesses...And now, brethren, I wot that through ignorance ye did it, as did also your rulers." Acts 3:14-15, 17

As the apostle Peter preached, he stated to the Jews that they had killed the prince of life, the Messiah that God had sent them. And they did this **THROUGH IGNORANCE!** Because they didn't know the prophecies about Jesus, because they didn't read through and love Scripture, because they didn't hold the Truth as important, they didn't know who their Messiah would be. Their hearts were fat with laziness and their ears and eyes were closed. The apostle Paul states the same thing:

> Men and brethren, children of the stock of Abraham, and whosoever among you feareth God, to you is the word of this salvation sent. For they that dwell at Jerusalem, and their rulers, because they knew him not, nor yet the voices of the prophets which are read every sabbath day, they have fulfilled them in condemning him. And though they found no cause of

> death in him, yet desired they Pilate that he should be
> slain. Acts 13:26-28

Because Israel did not understand what was written in the law, they didn't understand the foreshadowing, they didn't understand the things that the prophets had spoken to them, they ended up crucifying their Christ. They killed their savior. The mysteries were concealed from them because they did not have a strong enough desire to learn them! Because of this lack of knowledge, they ended up stumbling and killing Jesus. We need to learn from their example. Their disregard of the words of God and their apathy in searching it to know the Truth led them to making the greatest mistake ever made. What will we do?

We do NOT want to be like those who closed their ears and shut their eyes! We want to have open eyes and ears, ones that are searching through the Word of God, longing to make sense of what it is that He has said. These points are reinforced when we go to 1 Corinthians 2, another occurrence of the word "mystery."

> But we speak the wisdom of God in a mystery, even
> the hidden wisdom, which God ordained before the
> world unto our glory: which none of the princes of
> this world knew: for had they known it, they would
> not have crucified the Lord of glory. But as it is
> written, Eye hath not see, nor ear heard, neither have
> entered into the heart of men, the things which God
> hath prepared for them that love him. But God hath
> revealed them unto us by his Spirit: for the Spirit
> searcheth all things, yea, the deep things of God. 1
> Corinthians 2:7-10

This passage tells us almost the exact same thing as the one in Matthew! Remember what we saw there? The mystery had been revealed to the true believers who were willing to seek, but was hidden from the rest of the world. It is the same in this passage. He says that the mystery has been revealed! And when we look even deeper, we see that not only was the mystery revealed, but it was revealed to the faithful AND hidden to the world for the exact same reason as the mystery in Matthew. These are the two characteristics of the word "mystery." Again, to enumerate them, they are:

1. Scriptural mysteries can be understood.
2. They are understood by the faithful, because the true believers search through the Word and seek God's help in understanding it. The world never understands because they do not have the desire to look.

In 1 Corinthians we are told that the things spoken by Paul were "the wisdom of God in a mystery." It was "ordained before the world unto our glory." This was God's plan which was created before the foundation of the world (Matthew 25:34). Just as in the passage in Matthew, this was the mystery of the Kingdom—the mystery of God's plan. Yet Paul says that none of the princes of this world knew it! None of the princes of the world knew the promise of the Kingdom, none of them knew God's plan. Why? For the exact same reason as Matthew 13! None of them wanted to look deeper into it. It either seemed pointless to them to learn more, or they didn't want to take the time to go deeper into it. This is what Paul tells us of God's plan earlier in the same letter:

> But we preach Christ crucified, unto the Jews a <u>stumblingblock</u>, and unto the Greeks <u>foolishness</u>; but unto them which are called, both Jews and Greeks,

Christ the power of God, and the wisdom of God. Because the foolishness of God is wiser than men; and the weakness of God is stronger than men. 1 Corinthians 1:23-25

Paul preached Christ crucified. This was a stumbling block to the Jews and foolishness to the Greeks. It did not fit into the worldly "wisdom." It was something that just didn't make sense to them! This is the same with the gospel! The plan of God is foolishness with men! They don't care to look into it. Who wants to believe in a crucified Messiah, as the world would think? Who believes that Jesus will come and rule over this world? That all sounds like foolishness to the wise and learned man. To the people of this world, the Truth of the gospel seems totally wrong, it seems ignorant. That was the way that it was designed: it was designed to make people think, designed to make people stop and ask questions. It was designed to make people take God's book, the Bible, and probe even further into it until it does make sense. The cross isn't foolishness. The plan of God is not a stumbling block. It is clear and logical, but only once one actually searches to know what it means. Jesus spoke the parables so that people would have eyes and not see, and have ears and not hear— that seeing they might see and not perceive; that hearing they might hear and not understand. God's plan seemed like foolishness so that those who did not seek for understanding would just brush it off, so that it would remain a mystery to them. In fact, in our passage in 1 Corinthians 2, Paul goes on to explain this same thing.

The purpose of the beginning of 1 Corinthians 2 is to show that the world did not understand the plan of God. Paul uses two examples to prove this. The first example is the Jews. He shows that they didn't know the mystery of God because they killed their Messiah (1 Corinthians 2:8). The second example is a quote from Isaiah 64—"Eye hath not seen, nor ear heard, neither have entered into the heart of man, the things which God hath prepared for them that love him." This quote is interesting, because often you will hear this verse quoted to talk about the Kingdom of God! We are told that eye hath not seen nor ear heard what God will do in the Kingdom. It will be so amazing that we cannot even comprehend it. While this is true, Paul is trying to prove a different point. This is not what the passage is telling us. His line of argument is as follows: "No one knows God's mystery, which has been hidden throughout all ages. Here's some proof: if the Jews had known about it, they would not have killed Jesus. But, they didn't know what their Messiah was supposed to do, so they got rid of Him. In addition, here's more proof from the Old Testament: no one has seen, no one has heard about the thing that God prepares for those who love Him! No one in this world knows about it (it can be seen that this is what the apostle meant with his quote of Isaiah 64 by going back to Isaiah and reading the context of the verse quoted). Everyone is wallowing in ignorance!" BUT, as he goes on to say, God has revealed this plan to us, the true believers, those who have chosen to have the mind of the Spirit, those who try to think as God thinks. God has showed us the mystery because we have filled our minds with His word. God shows the mystery to people who seek to know and earnestly set out to understand. This is told to us all throughout the Bible.

"Yea, if thou criest after knowledge, and liftest up thy voice for understanding; <u>if thou seekest her as silver, and searchest for her as for hid treasures;</u> then shalt thou understand the fear of the LORD, and find the knowledge of God." Proverbs 2:3-5

We are counseled to seek for understanding as though it were silver or hidden treasure. We are to hold to an understanding of God's Truth as something that is extremely precious, something that is a treasure to us!

"Get wisdom, get understanding: forget it not, and she shall preserve thee: love her, and she shall keep thee. Wisdom is the principal thing; therefore get wisdom: and with all thy getting get understanding." Proverbs 4:5-7

With all of your getting get understanding. Earnestly strive with all of your effort, praying to God to understand.

"Receive my instruction, and not silver; and knowledge rather than choice gold. For wisdom is better than rubies; and all the things that may be desired are not to be compared to it." Proverbs 8:10-11

Again we see the same idea. Wisdom is better than gold. It is something that we should long to have.

"I love them that love me; and those that seek me early shall find me." Proverbs 8:17

This is wisdom personified in Proverbs. She states: those that seek me early shall find me. Those who are willing to wake up early, who are willing to give up other things in order to understand, those kind of people will find her. They will learn Truth.

"And I say unto you, Ask, and it shall be given you; seek, and ye shall find; knock, and it shall be opened unto you." Luke 11:9-10

If we care enough to understand that we ask God for guidance, and then go leaf through our Bibles, sincerely allowing it to teach us instead of making it conform to our thoughts, then true knowledge will be given to us. Ask and it shall be given you.

"If any of you lack wisdom, let him ask of God, that giveth to all men liberally, and upbraideth not; and it shall be given him." James 1:5

Ask God and He will help you to understand.

"It is the glory of God to conceal a thing: but the honor of kings is to search out a matter." Proverbs 25:2

Out of all of these verses, this one is my favorite. "It is the glory of God to conceal a thing." God will hide His Truth all throughout the Bible so that we have to search for it! And it is the honor of kings to search out a matter! It is an honor to be able to open up the Scriptures and look for the gospel. Have you ever wondered why God didn't just write down the gospel and the way in which He wanted us to live, why He didn't just write it down on a single piece of paper and tell us to learn it and live it? Instead He wrote the Bible, a book with over 1000 pages, filled with prophecies and stories, laws, and letters. He did this as a sifting process. He is looking for those people who are willing to read through the Bible and fill their minds with it. He is looking for those people who study His Scriptures, who look for the Truth throughout it. It is His glory to conceal a matter, and it is an honor for us to search out what He has written.

All of these verses teach us the same lesson. There are things that we don't innately know, understanding and wisdom that we do not innately have, but God is willing to reveal it. For those people who are willing to accept His mystery, who are willing to accept His wisdom, it is no longer a mystery anymore. We have to long for it, search for it, and receive it when we find it. But that is the key! For us, there should be no Scriptural mysteries! God has revealed them and it is up to us to ask Him for strength and understanding, and then to pick up His Book and search. He has shown the answer. If we do not know what that answer is, then the fault lies with us. It is our job to search for it, it is our job to accept it when we find it. This is the duty of kings!

As it is expressed in Deuteronomy:

"The secret things belong unto the LORD our God: but those things which are revealed belong unto us and to our children for ever, that we may do all the words of this law." Deuteronomy 29:29

God has revealed many things to us through His Word, and it is our job to go through that Word and possess those things as our own. They have been given to us. That's why Paul repeatedly referred to the gospel as "my gospel," (Romans 2:16; 2 Timothy 2:8) because he had taken it as his own—it belonged to him. It wasn't a mystery, but something that he loved, something that he owned, something that he understood.

Christianity today has put itself in an unsteady position because of their reliance on the word "mystery" to explain their view of God. As we have seen, Scripture plainly shows us that a mystery is something that is REVEALED to the BELIEVERS and not to the WORLD. Essentially, modern Christianity is condemning itself as "the world" because of their reliance on this word "mystery." This is something that we <u>must</u> understand before we move on. "Mystery" is used by the churches today as a crutch, to cause people to stop asking questions and to stop searching for answers. This is the same attitude that the Jews had before, where they were condemned for their lack of knowledge, where they crucified their Savior because of ignorance. God wants us to understand who He is and He calls us to search through His Word and pray to Him for understanding in order to learn. It isn't acceptable to say that the Trinity is a mystery and move on, in fact, it is condemning because it says "I have closed my eyes and closed my ears to the Word. Even though I don't understand how Jesus could have been God and yet been seen, since no man has seen God at any time (1 John 4:12), I'm not going to look into it. Even though my understanding of God contradicts certain things that are said in Scripture, I won't ask anymore questions." God wants us to know Him. May we then embark on this study together, with hearts and minds that long to know, with ears that are open to Scripture. May we seek to open up our BIBLES, and to see the TRUTH about God. As we approach this subject of God manifestation, let us remember that God will reveal the mystery to us if we search. Let us remember that this is what He wants us to do. He wants us to look, and He has purposefully hidden the Truth about Himself so that we have to search it out.

Knowing Our Creator

So then, let us go on to search through these pages together so that the relationship between God and Christ, which may seem to be a mystery, will be unveiled and we will see the gospel in its fulness. Let us take the next few pages of this chapter to consider God, different aspects of Him, and His character. A supreme aspect of God is told to us in Isaiah 45.

> I am the LORD, and there is none else, there is no God beside me: I girded thee, though thou hast not known me: that they may know from the rising of the sun, and from the west, that there is none beside me. I am the LORD, and there is none else. I form the light, and create darkness: I make peace, and create evil: I the LORD do all these things. Isaiah 45:5-7

He is the Almighty God. There is no power apart from Him. He makes the light. He makes the darkness. Everything that takes place in this world happens because He allows it, even the disaster ("evil" in the KJV). This is an essential point for us to understand. He is THE God of the Universe. There is no other. Only He gets the glory and the praise. Jesus expresses this same point as he speaks to a scribe about "the greatest commandment":

"And Jesus answered him, The first of all commandments is, Hear, O Israel; The Lord our God is one Lord: and thou shalt love the Lord thy God with all thy heart, and with all thy soul, and with all thy mind, and with all thy strength: this is the first commandment." Mark 12:29-30

This is a powerful set of verses. A scribe had come to him and asked "which is the first commandment of all?" Immediately, our Lord's response is "Hear, O Israel; The Lord our God is one Lord: and thou shalt love the Lord thy God with all thy heart, and with all thy soul, and with all thy mind, and with all thy strength." This was the greatest commandment; and it was bursting over with emphasis on God! It emphasized that they were to give Him all of their love, but even more, it emphasized that HE WAS ONE! This was such an important emphasis because if our God were more than one, if He were two, or three, then the praise that we would give to Him would be split up. Imagine it like this: say that you were an ancient Egyptian, and you had one hour in which you could worship God every day (basically just like condensing a lifetime). In addition, you had three gods that you worshipped, the god of rain, the god of sleep, and the god of the sun. How would you split up your hour to worship them? I would probably split my hour into thirds, worshipping each god for 20 minutes. However, what if it turned out that only one of those gods truly existed—that there was only one god? Unfortunately, you would have spent two thirds of your hour worshipping nothing and only giving one third of your worship to a real god. This is the reason that Jesus here emphasizes that God is one; because as one, He can then be worshipped for our entire hour, for all of our life! We are told that He is ONE and that we need to love Him with ALL, every single bit of our heart, every single bit of our mind, and with every part of our strength. God is ONE, He is the ONLY God. All worship, thanksgiving, praise, and love should ultimately end with Him. This aspect of who God is, His divine rulership over everything and limitless power, fits perfectly together with His purpose in this creation.

THE PURPOSE OF CREATION

God's purpose is to lift up His name. It is to honor Himself. This is the entire point of our existence. If fact, it is the entire purpose of the Bible, of creation. God's purpose in creating man was to bring glory to Himself. He is the amazing, supreme Creator of all things and the world revolves around Him.

"Thou art worthy, O Lord, to receive glory and honor and power: for thou hast created all things, and <u>for thy pleasure they are and were created</u>." Revelation 4:11

All things were created for GOD's pleasure. God created things here on this globe so that all of the earth would one day worship Him and all show forth His awesome character. Here's the important thing for us to recognize when looking at this purpose: creating everything for His pleasure may seem conceited or self-centered, but it isn't. His purpose is far from that; God is not conceited or full of Himself; total praise is just what He deserves. Can ANYONE or ANYTHING in this world claim that they are perfect, as He is? This is the lesson that Job was taught. No matter what, God is always right, and He deserves praise just for that fact alone. He rules over everything and He declares what is right and what is wrong. He is the source of all authority, and no one can argue with Him. God's purpose isn't about conceit, it isn't because He has a complex and has to be praised, but the fact is that He DESERVES it. He deserves to have every single part of His creation worship Him. In addition to deserving this praise, worshipping God is the best thing for us as well. Seeking to be like Him is the way that we can be given eternal life and the Kingdom! It is the way that we can escape sin! Learning to praise and do everything for God's pleasure is the best thing for us. Thus, God's purpose is good because it is RIGHT and second because it is LOVING towards us. All of creation is all about God. This is said to us repeatedly throughout the Bible. The purpose of God is to fill the earth with His glory. Many of us may be familiar with this verse:

"But as truly as I live, all the earth shall be filled with the glory of the LORD." Numbers 14:21

God plans to fill this EARTH with His glory. He wants to fill this earth with people who have His character, who follow His will, who understand His greatness and joy in it.

Here are some other verses that state the same thing:

"By whom also we have access by faith into this grace wherein we stand, and rejoice in <u>hope of the glory of God</u>." Romans 5:2

The hope of the gospel is the glory of God!

"And when all things shall be subdued unto him, then shall the Son also himself be subject unto him that put all things under him, that God may be all in all." 1 Corinthians 15:28

After Christ has subdued all things, when all people accept His rule on this earth, then Jesus will be subject to God, and God will be ALL IN ALL. His glory will fill the earth.

"Blessed be the LORD God, the God of Israel, who only doeth wondrous thing. And blessed be his glorious name for ever: and let the whole earth be filled with his glory; Amen, and Amen." Psalm 72:18-19

All creation is here for the glory of God. One day, all of this earth will be filled with that glory.

The Character of the Father

We now delve into looking at the character of God, which brings us to the doorstep of God manifestation. Ultimately, being able to understand this concept of God manifestation not only allows us to see the more physical aspects of God—such as His oneness—and to treasure the relationship between Him and His Son, but it also allows us to truly see the FATHER's character. Through those who manifest Him, we will be able to see God's mercy, we will see His patience, we will see His justice.

God's character being shown through God manifestation is a key thing for us to notice, because the Father greatly desires for us to know His character. He wants to have a personal relationship with us in which He intimately knows us and we intimately know Him. He wants us to see His character and realize its beauty. He wants us to understand His characteristics and how He thinks. As He says in Jeremiah:

> Thus saith the LORD, Let not the wise man glory in his wisdom, neither let the mighty man glory in his might, let not the rich man glory in his riches: but let him that glorieth glory in this, that he understandeth and knoweth me, that I am the LORD which exercise lovingkindness, judgment, and righteousness, in the earth: for in these things I delight, saith the LORD. Jeremiah 9:23-24

God wants us to understand who He is, to know what He loves and what He hates! He does not want to remain a mystery to us. He wants us to know how He interacts with people and creation so that we can follow in His path. He wants us to see how He loves and cares for His son, how He supports His son, so that we can learn to do that for our children. He wants us to know the passion with which He hates sin so that we can abhor the evil and love the good. God longs and powerfully wants us to know who He is.

Understanding God manifestation opens the door for us to not only understand the relationship between the Father and His son, but also to see the Father's character in action. And that is what we will do in the next few chapters.

THE MYSTERY OF GOD

A Summary

1. When discussing the Trinity, many people refer to it as a

    _____ _____.

2. What are the two main characteristics of a mystery according to Scripture?

        a.

        b.

3. How many times is the word "mystery" (including "mysteries") used in the Bible?

4. Why did Jesus speak in parables?

5. Multiple choice:

        Why did Israel end up crucifying their Messiah?

           a. Because they thought that they were fulfilling prophecy

           b. Because they didn't think that they needed a Messiah

           c. Because they knew too much

           d. Because they were ignorant about what God had said

6. <u>Why</u> is it that eye hath not seen, neither ear heard the things which God has prepared for those who love Him?

7. God purposefully hides things throughout the Bible. True/False

8. List three verses that teach us that we have to search through the Scripture to find Truth.

    _____

    _____

    _____

23

9. How does God feel about us using the word "mystery" to describe something that He has revealed but we do not understand?

10. What is God's purpose?

11. Give a verse to prove this: _____

Answers:

1. Mystery
2. a. Scriptural Mysteries can be understood
   b. They are understood by the faithful, because the faithful seek them out. The world does not understand.
3. 27 times
4. He spoke in parables to purposefully confuse people, to hide the message so that listeners would have to search for the meaning.
5. d.
6. Because no one ever looked to find out what God has in store for those who love Him.
7. True
8. Any of the verses from pgs. 12-14
9. He is not pleased. He wants us to search!
10. To fill the earth with His glory.
11. Numbers 14:21 or any of the other verses on pg. 20

CHAPTER 2

GOD MANIFESTATION AND THE NAME

Have you ever had something go wrong with your computer? Maybe your hard drive shut down, or your CD drive would no longer recognize disks. Whatever the problem was, you probably decided to call customer support. In my case, if this were to happen, I might call up a local computer repair shop. Let's follow this scenario:

The phone rings three times and an employee answers, saying, "Friendly Computers, this is Robert." From this point on, the person on the other line of the phone represents "Friendly Computers" to me. He would answer my questions about my computer and hopefully convey the customer-friendly attitude of the company to me. However, he also might not. Maybe that morning he had woken up after a terrible dream, stepped on his dog as he was getting out of bed, and cut himself shaving. Because of those things, he might be feeling incredibly frustrated and say to me, "Listen. I understand that your computer will not shut down. That's just too bad. Maybe if you didn't treat it like trash it would work." In that case, I would be frustrated as well. "I do take care of my computer…" I would think. And because of how he spoke to me, and his unhelpful attitude, my opinion of Friendly Computers' customer service would greatly decrease;

and not only my opinion of their customer service, but of their whole company. I would probably think "Wow. That was one of the worst phone calls I've had in a long time. What a rude employee, and he wasn't even helpful! I don't want to deal with that company anymore. I'm calling someone else next time." Therefore, in conveying to me a bad attitude, Robert would not be doing his job. Rather than representing the company to me, rather than showing me their character, he would be misrepresenting them. He had the reputation of Friendly Computers on his shoulders. The company's name was at stake and it was just tarnished.

In the same way as a company, God uses representatives to show us His character and His name. Robert was able to answer the phone, saying, "Friendly Computers, this is Robert." He was not Friendly Computers —he was not the company itself, but a representative of it. As we will see, God also gives His representatives His name. They are not actually Him, but can be called by the name of God. And just as with the computer company, these representatives can either truly show people who He is, or they can misrepresent Him. They can choose to help people understand the Father through their actions, or they can choose to make people think that He is horrible. They can make people think that He is loving and just, or that He is indifferent about them, and callous. God is shown to the rest of the world through people who bear His name. A Biblical example of this representation occurs in the book of Esther.

"And he wrote in the king Ahasuerus' name, and sealed it with the king's ring, and sent letters by posts on horseback, and riders on mules, camels, and young dromedaries." Esther 8:10

This verse is speaking about Mordecai the Jew. In the story of Esther, the Prime Minister of Persia, named Haman, tried to have all of the Jews annihilated. In order to do this, he issued a decree ordering that all of the inhabitants of the empire could kill the Jews and take their possessions on a certain day of the month. Esther and Mordecai, who are Jews, found out about the decree, and created a plan to tell the king about it and Haman's trickery. The king was not pleased. After Haman was slain, Mordecai was exalted to Haman's position as one of the chief princes and was given Haman's authority and possessions. Unfortunately, even after Haman had been killed, his decree to kill all of the Jews still stood. With the king's permission, Mordecai and Esther wrote a new decree which reversed the one that Haman made and allowed all of the Jews to defend themselves when their enemies came to kill them. Mordecai signed the decree as "King Ahasuerus," because he was the king's representative. He held the king's signet ring, he possessed the king's authority, and could therefore sign in his name. Just as with Friendly Computers, and just as this verse, God uses representatives in this same way. They hold His authority, they work on His behalf, and they seek to reveal Him to the world. This system of representation and revealing can be called God manifestation. Another definition for "manifest" is "reveal." God manifestation is the revealing of God. As I mentioned before, God manifestation, or the revealing of God, is done through His name-bearing representatives, just as the attitude of Friendly Computers can be shown through their name-bearing employees. Those who are to "manifest God" are to reveal God in their actions and thoughts. They are to show people His character, or show them His name. And as we will see, there is a very strong link between God's name and who He is.

THE SIGNIFICANCE OF GOD'S NAME

This link between God's name and His character is shown to us in Exodus chapter 34:

> And the LORD descended in the cloud, and stood with him there, and proclaimed the name of the LORD. And the LORD passed by before him, and proclaimed, The LORD, The LORD God, merciful and gracious, longsuffering, and abundant in goodness and truth, keeping mercy for thousands, forgiving iniquity and transgression and sin, and that will by no means clear the guilty; visiting the iniquity of the fathers upon the children, and upon the children's children, unto the third and to the fourth generation. Exodus 34:5-7

These verses give us a description of who God is; basically, His character. He is merciful, gracious, slow to anger, yet still just! This is a beautiful list of characteristics. If you have not already done so, these are wonderful verses to commit to memory.

Now if we turn our focus to the beginning of our quotation, we will see an interesting connection. We see that in these verses, God "proclaimed the name of the LORD." But what part of this quotation is the "name of the LORD"? Is it when God says "the LORD, the LORD," or could we say that "the name of the LORD" is referring to EVERYTHING that God proclaims here, including His character? I believe that we can. Just from reading the verse, it seems that the statement "and proclaimed the name of the LORD" is almost a summation of everything that was to come. If we choose to pursue this understanding, we see that it is very consistent with Scripture teaching. When God proclaimed "the name of the LORD," what He really did was explain who He was, He revealed His character. So it follows then that the Father's name and His characteristics are closely related. This is shown throughout the rest of the Bible. Take a look at the following three verses, which all mention God's name:

"I will praise the LORD according to his righteousness: and will sing praise <u>to the name of the LORD</u> most high." Psalm 7:17

"O Lord, I beseech thee, let now thine ear be attentive to the prayer of thy servant, and to the prayer of thy servants, who desire <u>to fear thy name</u>: and prosper, I pray thee, thy servant this day, and grant him mercy in the sight of this man. For I was the king's cupbearer." Nehemiah 1:11

"I will also leave in the midst of thee an afflicted and poor people, and they shall <u>trust in the name of the LORD</u>." Zephaniah 3:12

When we look at these three passages (and there are many more in Scripture), we see that they all mention God's name. It can be understood, when reading these verses, that when His name is mentioned, they are not speaking of His actual name, Yahweh, but rather Who that name represents. The verses are speaking of God Himself, of His character. They are talking about Him and who He is. When Zephaniah speaks of the people trusting in God's name, he doesn't mean that the people will trust in the characters and letters of God's name, but that they will trust in God! They will trust in His power, in His faithfulness, in His mercy. We see this same use of God's name in Psalm 20. This psalm speaks of all of the many things that are accomplished by God's name, and all of the things that it can do. But God's name is a word that is made up of letters, and it literally cannot do those things mentioned. However, the One that it represents can! Sometimes, when Scripture mentions God's name, it is actually speaking of Him individually, or who He is. In other words, the people who delight to fear that name, as Nehemiah said, fear what His name represents. It represents Him and His plan! It represents who He is.

We find this connection between someone's name and character in modern society as well. If you were reading the newspaper, or watching the news, and one of the articles or programs mentioned "Bill Gates," what would you think of? Would your first thoughts be about the word "Bill" and its various meanings, such as a duck bill, or maybe a dollar bill; and about the word "Gates," and how "gates" are placed in front of expensive houses or gated communities? No at all! Instead, if you heard the name "Bill Gates," you would probably think of a very wealthy man who wears glasses and founded Microsoft. Thus, the name "Bill Gates" does not actually refer to the specific words of his name, but rather who he is and his characteristics. In the same way, as we have seen through Exodus 34 and the other verses, God's name is associated with His attributes.

There is a link between God's name and His character. His name means mercy, grace, longsuffering, goodness, truthfulness, sinlessness, all powerfulness. God's name is who He is; He is His character. Because of this, God's representatives are called by His name and strive to show people that name by showing His characteristics. Possessing this character and this name is the essence of God manifestation. Once we are CALLED by His name, or associated with it, we become associated with God. We become God's representatives, commissioned to show forth His character. Notice, however, that we don't actually POSSESS His name, because if we did, then that would mean that we would possess His perfect character and nature. As we progress in this subject and relate it to Jesus and ourselves, we will see that possessing that name, that beautiful character, is what we hope to have happen to us eventually. When that name is given to us, then it will be ours and we will be able to be true, perfect, representatives of God. When we are given that name, we will become flawless representatives of Him. As we look at the example of the angels, Jesus, and eventually us, we will be able to see this enacted. But, before delving into the work of the angels, we will first seek to understand more about God's personal name.

HEBREW MEANING OF GOD'S NAME

When you are trying to get to know someone, it is important for you to know their name. For obvious reasons, knowing someone's name will help you become closer to them. In our case, knowing God's name will help us come closer to Him, because it will give us better understanding of passages that we read in our Bibles. And so, we will learn how to recognize His personal name when we read it. There are a number of different words in the Bible that refer to God, just as we have many different names and titles by which people refer to us. For example, I could be called by many different names: Mr. Hensley, Jason, a Christadelphian from California, among others. In this chapter, we will be looking at two of God's names or titles. First, we will see His personal name, and then next we will examine His title.

When the Bible uses the words "The LORD," with "Lord" being completely capitalized, God's personal name is being used. God's personal name is "Yahweh;" some also refer to it as "Jehovah," but Yahweh is supposed to be more correct. When we read "the LORD" it is similar to someone calling me Jason Hensley. This is God's personal name; it is not a title. It is unique. When the Bible says "the LORD," it is speaking of the Father. The only other times when the word is not used of God, personally, is when others are manifesting or revealing Him. They are His representatives and can be called by His name because it is their job to show people what that name means.

It is interesting to note that this word, "Yahweh," is only used in the Old Testament, since the New Testament was written in Greek (thus, it would not use Hebrew words). The Greek references for the Father are a bit more basic, but also confusing, since He does not have his own personal name. Rather, He is called "God" and "Lord," which are used to refer to other things as well, not just the Father. Nevertheless, when we read "the LORD" in the Old Testament, we are reading God's name. Here are two examples of "the LORD" being used in the Old Testament, so that we can see how the word looks and is used in Scripture:

"Now Abraham was old, and well stricken in age: and the LORD had blessed Abraham in all things." Genesis 24:1

"Praise the LORD, for the LORD is good; sing praises unto his name; for it is pleasant." Psalm 135:3

"The LORD" is God's personal name, so these instances either refer to Yahweh Himself or beings that are representing Him. Now that we understand what it means when we read "the LORD," let us spend a bit of time looking at God's title, the Hebrew word for "God."

Often when we are speaking about Yahweh, the God of Israel, we just tend to call Him "God." Thus, some people tend to stumble when they see this term applied to Christ because they feel as though it is the LORD's title, and His title only. Since they see the title applied to Christ at times, they tend to believe that Jesus must be Yahweh because he is called God. As we are studying God manifestation and God's name being given to His representatives, we will also see that it is possible for others to legitimately be called "God." The reason for this is that the Hebrew word does not just mean "God," but can also mean a few other things, such as a "powerful being." This word "God" is the Hebrew word "elohim."

Strong's Concordance and Lexicon (a Biblical dictionary of Hebrew and Greek) defines this as:

H430
'elohiym
el-o-heem'
Plural of H433; gods in the ordinary sense; but specifically used (in the plural thus, especially with the article) of the supreme God; occasionally applied by way of deference to magistrates; and sometimes as a superlative: - angels, X exceeding, God (gods) (-dess, -ly), X (very) great, judges, X mighty.

Because "elohim" can mean "powerful being" it can most definitely be applied to angels, but sometimes it is also applied to men (as can be seen by Exodus 21 and 22, which use the word "elohim" to refer to the judges). This is why the

Bible occasionally speaks of Yahweh as the greatest among the gods! It isn't because there actually are multiple deities in the universe, but we are being told that among everything in this world that is mighty, God is the greatest and most powerful, none can stand before Him. Here are a few examples of verses like this:

"Who is like unto thee, O LORD, among the gods? who is like thee, glorious in holiness, fearful in praises, doing wonders?" Exodus 15:11

"For the LORD is a great God, and a great King above all gods." Psalm 95:3

God is greater than the mighty ones of this world, greater than the idols, greater than those who believe that they are mighty.

Just like other words (as we will speak of in chapter 6), "elohim" can have multiple meanings. Sometimes it is referring plainly to Yahweh, other times it is speaking of mighty ones, which includes the angels, and sometimes it can refer to Jesus. What we must learn from this is that when others are called "God," that does not necessarily mean that they are God Himself, but could just possibly mean that they are powerful. The definition must be chosen based on the context of the word. "Elohim" means "mighty ones," and although it is used of God Himself, it is also used to refer to others who are not God. However, God's name, "the LORD" applies only to Him and His representatives. So when others are called by His name, this is a very different situation. The amazing thing that we will see in this study of God manifestation is that people and angels can be called "the LORD," God's personal name. As we read through the next chapter, we will see angels who are called "Yahweh", not because they are Him, but because they are His ambassadors.

GOD MANIFESTATION AND THE NAME

A Summary

1. God reveals Himself to people through representatives who bear His name. True/False

2. What is this form of representation called?

3. God's name and His character are closely connected. Give three verses which prove this.

_____   _____

_____

4. What is God's name?

5. When someone is called "God" that automatically means that they are the LORD. True/False

ANSWERS:

1. True
2. God manifestation
3. Any of the verses from pgs. 29-30
4. Yahweh
5. False

CHAPTER 3

FOLLOWING THE ANGELS

They are the messengers of God, going about to do His bidding. They speak His words, follow His will, and perform actions for Him. Angels are the representatives of God. Throughout this chapter, we will see how angels, just as Friendly Computers' employee (chapter 2), can carry the name of God and act on His behalf. We will do this by studying six different incidents in which angels were God's representatives, and even called "Yahweh." We will see that they could be called this because they were working for Him, because they were following His will and acting on His behalf. With this understanding, we will be able to see how certain "mysteries" of Scripture become more apparent.

1 – THE FLIGHT OF HAGAR

Many promises had been made to Abram, promises which included a seed who would possess the land. Despite the fact that his wife Sarai had not yet been able to have children, Abram still believed what his God had told him. The years went by and still Sarai did not have a son. Her closed womb was troublesome, and thus Sarai came to Abram asking him to take Hagar, her Egyptian slave, as a wife and to try to have an heir through her. We know the end of the story. Because Hagar was able to have a son, she began to feel as though she were better than Sarai and despised her mistress. As her mistress, Sarai treated her firmly for her behavior, and Hagar ran away. While she was in the wilderness, one of God's angels appeared to her:

> And the angel of the LORD said unto her, I will multiply thy seed exceedingly, that it shall not be numbered for multitude. And the angel of the LORD said unto her, Behold, thou art with child, and shalt bear a son, and shalt call his name Ishmael; because the LORD hath heard thy affliction. And he will be a wild man; his hand will be against every man, and every man's hand against him; and he shall dwell in the presence of all his brethren. And she called the name of the LORD that spake unto her, Thou God seest me: for she said, Have I also here looked after him that seeth me? Genesis 16:10-13

Take some time to examine this passage and then ask yourself "Who was it that spoke to Hagar?" It was an angel of the LORD—God's angel. Now, go through these four verses and note all of the phrases and words that would indicate to us that the angel was speaking God's words. After you have looked through the quotation, here are the things that I have noticed:

1. The angel actually said "<u>I will</u> surely multiply your offspring." This seems as though it would have been what God said to Hagar, speaking through the angel.
2. After the angel is finished speaking, the Scripture tells us that Hagar "called the name of <u>the LORD</u> who spoke to her." Scripture tells us that "Yahweh" spoke to her.

You might have found some other indications as well, which just serve to reinforce this point. The angel who spoke to Hagar could come and speak God's words for Him. He was a representative of God, and so could speak the words of God to Hagar. Because he was God's representative, it was as though God had spoken the words, and so Scripture writes, "she called the name of the LORD that spake unto her." It was Yahweh who had spoken to her through the angel. Angels are God's ambassadors, and we will see even further their ability to represent God by seeing them called by His name, "Yahweh."

2 – THE DESTRUCTION OF SODOM AND GOMORRAH

One chapter after the incident with Hagar, Yahweh changed Abram's name to Abraham and Sarai's name to Sarah. Some time after the name change, Abraham is visited by the LORD. This visit begins in Genesis 18.

> And the LORD appeared unto him in the plains of Mamre: and he sat in the tent door in the heat of the day; and he lift up his eyes and looked, and, lo, three men stood by him: and when he saw them, he ran to meet them from the tent door, and bowed himself toward the ground. Genesis 18:1-2

We see here that Yahweh appeared to Abraham. If you read through the passage you will notice that "the LORD" is referred to often, so we can be sure that Scripture wanted us to understand that it was Yahweh Himself who visited Abraham. Here is an example of this:

"And the LORD said unto Abraham, Wherefore did Sarah laugh, saying, Shall I of a surety bear a child, which am old?" Genesis 18:13

The LORD was there speaking to him. This is God's name, so it would make sense that it was Him who was there speaking to Abraham. He was there. He appeared to Abraham, Abraham and Sarah prepared a meal for Him and He ate with Abraham, speaking to him about the promises. However, as we read through the chapter, God says something fairly striking, something that does not seem to fit with our understanding of God at all.

"And the LORD said, Because the cry of Sodom and Gomorrah is great, and because their sin is very grievous; I will go down now, and see whether they have done altogether according to the cry of it, which is come unto me; and if not, I will know." Genesis 18:20-21

Look through these verses. What is strange about them if it was literally Yahweh who had been speaking to Abraham?

"I will go down now, and see whether they have done altogether according to the cry of it, which is come unto me; and if not, I will know." If this is actually the LORD, then this saying seems very strange. It is written of our God that "there is no searching of His understanding" (Isaiah 40:28) and "thou knowest my downsitting and mine uprising, thou understandest my thought afar off" (Psalm 139:20). God knows everything that is taking place, for His understanding is limitless! Unless we understand this as speaking of representatives of God who were bearing His name, something seems very wrong. How could God not know what was going on in Sodom? Why would He have to go and see if things were as bad as He had heard? He would have known already! The best way to reconcile the omniscience of God and this passage is to say that something was there representing Yahweh. Could they be angels? Let us continue to follow the story:

"And the men turned their faces from thence, and went toward Sodom: but Abraham stood yet before the LORD." Genesis 18:22

Thus, one of these men stood before Abraham and spoke to him. From there came the dialogue in which Abraham sought to reason with God. He pleaded to God to save Sodom if 50 righteous are found therein, then dropped down to 40, then moved down to 30, and so on. The other two men went down to Sodom as "the LORD" (remember that God had said that he would go to Sodom?). So, all three of the men represented God and were called by His name. The two men went down to Sodom as "the LORD" in order to fulfill what God had said in verses 20-21. Then, the other man stayed before Abraham to speak to him and this man is called "Yahweh" as well (verse 22).

If the story just ended there, we would only be able to speculate about who these "men" were. All three of them were called "the LORD," and yet they were not omniscient. It is probably very tempting for many Trinitarians to look at this passage and try to squeeze the Trinity into it. However, the story does not end there; in fact, we can follow the two men who left for Sodom. When we do that, a very powerful revelation is opened up.

"And there came <u>two angels</u> to Sodom at even; and Lot sat in the gate of Sodom: and Lot seeing them rose up to meet them; and he bowed himself with his face toward the ground." Genesis 19:1

TWO ANGELS! It is just as we had thought earlier when God had said "I will go down now and see whether they have done altogether according to the cry of it." In this passage, the ones called "Yahweh" were three angels bearing God's name. In Genesis 18:21, two men left to go to Sodom. In Genesis 19:1, two angels arrived at Sodom. Do we need a stronger connection? These three men that visited Abraham were angels who were called by God's name! They bore His name as His representatives. They were acting on His behalf.

A QUICK SUMMARY

We have now looked at two incidents in which angels were God's representatives, even being called "Yahweh" in the last example. I find God manifestation through the angels to be a truly fascinating concept. The logic of the case is wonderful, and the Scriptural proof is abundant. In addition, these are not things that you would notice just casually reading through the chapters. It is just as it was said in the first chapter: God hides the truths about Himself and wants us to dig deep to find them. It is like buried treasure that we have seek out.

Finding this treasure, we learn that as a messenger or ambassador of God, an angel can essentially speak God's words for Him, can act on His behalf, and can make decisions with His authority. It is important for us that we understand this concept, because it will be a powerful help in our understanding of Jesus' relationship with God. The next example of representative angels that we will see takes place throughout the life of Jacob, the grandson of Abraham.

3 - JACOB'S ANGEL

This example begins with Jacob living in Egypt, speaking to his son Joseph.

> And he blessed Joseph, and said, <u>God</u>, before whom my fathers Abraham and Isaac did walk, <u>the God</u> which fed me all my life long unto this day, <u>the Angel</u> which redeemed me from all evil, bless the lads; and let my name be named on them, and the name of my fathers Abraham and Isaac; and let them grow into a multitude in the midst of the earth. Genesis 48:15-16

Here Jacob was blessing the children of Joseph. If you examine the words that Jacob speaks here, you will notice a slight change in the way that he refers to the one who was watching over him. First, he begins by speaking of the God of his fathers, the God of Abraham and Isaac. Then, still describing the same being, says "the angel which redeemed me from all evil." He is speaking of the God who fed him all of his life, and then suddenly, he calls that same God "the Angel which redeemed me from all evil." The word "God" in the beginning is the word "elohim" that we had studied earlier, now applied to an angel! Here, Jacob is speaking of an angel who followed him, an angel who watched over him, and angel who provided for him all throughout his life and he calls that angel "God" or "mighty one." This serves to illustrate what was said in chapter 2 about the word "elohim." When we see something referred to as "God" it does not have to mean that the thing referred to is part of the deity! Instead, as it is here, the word could be speaking of the being as one who is mighty. As we now take a trip back through the life of Jacob to examine this angel, we will see that Jacob's angel was called "God" many times, and also actually called "the LORD" or

"Yahweh" throughout these experiences. The first experience that we will observe is based off an incident at Bethel.

> And he dreamed, and behold a ladder set up on the earth, and the top of it reached to heaven: and behold the angels of God ascending and descending on it. And, behold, the LORD stood above it, and said, I am the LORD God of Abraham thy father, and the God of Isaac: the land whereon thou liest, to thee will I give it, and to thy seed. Genesis 28:12-13

You are probably familiar with this story, commonly known as Jacob's ladder. Jacob lay down in Bethel with a rock as his pillow. While he was sleeping, he dreamed about a ladder that reached forth from the earth, all the way up to heaven. On this ladder, he saw angels ascending and descending, going from heaven to earth and from earth to heaven. Above the ladder, Jacob saw Yahweh—he saw "the LORD"—who then spoke to him, saying "I am the LORD God of Abraham thy father, and the God of Isaac…" Jacob saw the LORD and the LORD called Himself "Yahweh." This incident took place early in Jacob's life in the place called Bethel (verse 19). Let us then venture three chapters further, when Jacob called together his wives Rachel and Leah, telling them that it was time for them to leave their father's household, where the three of them lived. As part of his message to them, he said:

> And the angel of God spake unto me in a dream, saying, Jacob: and I said, Here am I. And he said, Lift up now thine eyes, and see, all the rams which leap upon the cattle are ringstraked, speckled, and grisled: for I have seen all that Laban doeth unto thee. I am the God of Beth-el, where thou anointest the pillar, and where thou vowest a vow unto me: now arise, get

thee out from this land, and return unto the land of thy kindred. Genesis 31:11-13

You will notice that it was an angel that had spoken to Jacob. The angel called out his name, "Jacob," and then proceeded to speak to him about the animals of Laban. He then said, "I am the God of Bethel, where thou anointest the pillar, and where thou vowest a vow unto me." The angel just told Jacob that he was the God from Bethel! The ANGEL was the one that Jacob saw above the ladder, the one that Scripture called "the LORD"! He is the one that Jacob gazed upon during his dream! Is this not amazing? Again, this was probably the same angel that had followed Jacob all throughout his life, a personal angel, who, as Jacob said, "redeemed me from all evil." This was the angel that had taken care of him, the same one that he referred to in Genesis 48. This angel was called Yahweh. This angel bore God's name and authority because he was God's representative. Let us follow the angel through another incident in Jacob's life.

> And he said, Thy name shall be called no more Jacob, but Israel: for as a prince hast thou power with God and with men, and hast prevailed. And Jacob asked him, and said, Tell me, I pray thee, thy name. And he said, Wherefore is it that thou dost ask after my name? And he blessed him there. And Jacob called the name of the place Peniel: for I have seen God face to face, and my life is preserved. Genesis 32:28-30

Jacob was wrestling, struggling with a man and Jacob would not let him go until the man had blessed him. Finally, the man blessed him by changing his name. Israel was his new name, and its meaning was "Prince with God," hence, why the man told him "for as a prince hast thou power with God and with men, and hast prevailed." He had wrestled with the man, with "God," and had prevailed. In addition to this, Jacob also called the man "God," "for I have seen God face to face, and my life is preserved." It sounds as though he believed that he had seen Yahweh face to face. Within this selection of verses, two references are made to the man being God. However, let us turn to the prophets and we will see the true identity of this man.

"He took his brother by the heel in the womb, and by his strength he had power with God: yea, he had power over the angel, and prevailed: he wept, and made supplication unto him: he found him in Bethel, and there he spake with us." Hosea 12:3-4

These words in Hosea are looking back to the life of Jacob, speaking of his birth, when he grabbed Esau's heel in the womb (Genesis 25:26); then looking to the incident that we just read about in Genesis 32, wrestling with God. But now, Hosea adds something. "He had power with God: yea, he had power over the angel, and prevailed." Note the connection here between the words spoken when Jacob is given his new name and the words said here. The man told Jacob that he had power with God and had prevailed. Hosea says that Jacob had power with the angel and had prevailed. Again, from looking at the context we can see that Hosea is talking about the same incident as Genesis. The man that Jacob had struggled with was an angel! And in Genesis the angel is called God!

When we bring all of these experiences together, we see that there was an angel that was taking care of Jacob all throughout his life. We saw the angel in Bethel, we saw him struggling with Jacob just before he met Esau, and we saw Jacob reference him in Egypt. This angel was called God multiple times, and even once referred to as "the LORD." This was not because he was God, not by any means! But instead, the angel was a representative of God. He could do things for God, speak God's words, and be called by God's name.

4 - The Burning Bush

One of the strongest examples of God manifestation in the angels occurs at the burning bush. Many of us know the story very well. Moses was on Mount Horeb tending the flocks of his father-in-law, Jethro.

"And the <u>angel of the LORD</u> appeared unto him in a flame of fire out of the midst of a bush: and he looked, and, behold, the bush burned with fire, and the bush was not consumed. And Moses said, I will now turn aside, and see this great sight, why the bush is not burnt." Exodus 3:2-3

An angel of the LORD appeared to Moses. The angel appeared as a fiery, glowing heat that was burning on a bush, but not actually destroying it. This was an amazing scene! Imagine what it would be like for you if you were working at your job and suddenly you saw something taking place that you knew was impossible! This would be something that would catch your attention and draw you towards it, just as it did to Moses. An angel had just appeared to him.

As the chapter progresses, we see that God spoke to Moses out of the bush and charged him to bring the Israelites out of Egypt. But, after being rejected as their deliverer 40 years previously (see Acts 7:25-30), Moses was still hesitant.

He did not want to go back to the people who had cast him aside. He explained, "when I come to the elders of Israel and say 'the God of your fathers has sent me to you,' and they say 'what is His name?' what shall I say?" It is here at the burning bush that God revealed His memorial name "Yahweh" to Moses, "I will be whom I will be," as we understand it. And then, hidden throughout this narrative, as is often the case with examples of God manifestation, we see a connection that again calls an angel "Yahweh":

"Go, and gather the elders of Israel together, and say unto them, <u>The LORD God of your fathers, the God of Abraham, of Isaac, and of Jacob, appeared unto me</u>, saying, I have surely visited you, and seen that which is done to you in Egypt." Exodus 3:16

The angel had appeared to Moses in a flame of fire, verse 2. And now, speaking to him, God says, "Say unto them, 'The LORD God of your fathers, the God of Abraham, of Isaac, and of Jacob, appeared unto me." Who was it that had appeared to Moses according to verse 2? Who was it that appeared to Moses according to verse 16? Moses had seen an angel. The angel was fiery, was burning a bush, and yet God told him to tell the people that "Yahweh" had appeared to him, in fact, the God of Abraham, that of Isaac, and that of Jacob! This angel was called by God's memorial name! And we can understand why! The angel was a representative of God. Yahweh was there, through the angel!

As we proceed through this entire experience, Moses is still reluctant to return to Egypt. At the beginning of chapter 4, he states, "They will say, The LORD hath not appeared unto thee." From there God even reinforces this fact —He had appeared to Moses through an angel.

> And Moses answered and said, But, behold, they will not believe me, nor hearken unto my voice: for they will say, The LORD hath not appeared unto thee. And the LORD said unto him, What is that in thine hand? And he said, A rod. And he said, Cast it on the ground. And he cast it on the ground, and it became a serpent; and Moses fled from before it. And the LORD said unto Moses, Put forth thine hand, and take it by the tail. And he put forth his hand, and caught it, and it became a rod in his hand: That they may believe that the LORD God of their fathers, the God of Abraham, the God of Isaac, and the God of Jacob, hath appeared unto thee. Exodus 4:1-5

This time, Moses is actually given a sign to prove to people that Yahweh had appeared to him! For us, this is an emphasis that the angel who appeared to Moses could be called "the LORD." An angel appeared to Moses, told him to tell the elders that "Yahweh" had appeared to him, and then later gives him signs to prove to all of them that it was Yahweh that had actually appeared. This angel stood for God here because he was God to Moses. He was God's ambassador. Was he literally Yahweh? By no means, but he was His representative.

5 - THE GIVING OF THE LAW

When the law of Moses was given to Israel, another scene of God manifestation with the angels opens up. As we look at the New Testament quotations about the giving of the law, make a note in your mind of who it was that gave the law.

> This is that Moses, which said unto the children of Israel, A prophet shall the Lord your God raise up

unto you of your brethren, like unto me; him shall ye hear. This is he, that was in the church in the wilderness with <u>the angel which spake to him</u> in the mount Sina, and with our fathers: who received the lively oracles to give unto us. Acts 7:37-38

Stephen was a follower of Christ who defended the Truth before a restless body of Jews. These are part of his words as he stood before them. Throughout his testimony, he gave a fairly extensive history of Israel, showing how they had been strangers and wanderers all throughout their lives as a nation. He showed how God could be worshipped without a temple, and what true worship was really about. In the midst of this defense, he brought the Jews' minds back to Moses and the giving of the law. "This is he, that was in the church in the wilderness with the angel which spake to him in the mount Sina, and with our fathers: who received the lively oracles to give unto us." "Sina" is the same as "Sinai." The law was spoken both to Moses and to the people, or the "fathers" as Stephen specifically says. From Mount Sinai the fiery and blasting voice of an angel pierced through the sky. The law was heard throughout the congregation. It was an angel who had spoken to Israel, an angel who had spoken to Moses and given the law, "the angel which spake to him in the mount Sina, and with our fathers." This same conclusion is brought out in the letter to the Hebrews.

Therefore we ought to give the more earnest heed to the things which we have heard, lest at any time we should let them slip. For if <u>the word spoken by angels</u> was stedfast, and every transgression and disobedience received a just recompense of reward; How shall we escape, if we neglect so great salvation; which at the first began to be spoken by the Lord, and

was confirmed unto us by them that heard him.
Hebrews 2:1-3

The apostle is contrasting the law and the new covenant through Christ. The word spoken by angels (that is, the law) was steadfast, and every time it was broken a consequence was given. Therefore, since our calling (the new covenant) was given by Jesus himself, how much more will we be punished if we disobey it? The writer is proving the superiority of Jesus over the angels (see his arguments in Hebrews 1)! Notice also that the angels were the ones who gave the law. While this is not the point of these particular verses, this is the point on which we will focus. The law was given by angels. As we understand that, let us turn our attention to the actual law itself and what it tells us about its presenter.

In Exodus 20 we see the giving of the 10 commandments, a well-known part of the law. From what we looked at in the New Testament, we understand that the law was given and spoken by angels. Compare this to the first few words of Exodus 20, the actual account of where the law is being given:

"And God spake all these words, saying, I am the LORD thy God, which have brought thee out of the land of Egypt, out of the house of bondage." Exodus 20:1-2

Exodus tells us that God was speaking these things, and in addition to that, God says, "I am the LORD thy God." This again is another example of God manifestation through the angels that can only be discovered through careful study and comparing passages. The law was given by angels, and the angels who gave it were called "God" and said to the nation

"I am the LORD thy God"! As you turn a few chapters forward, you see the same thing. More laws were given, and as we read earlier they were given by angels. But, here is what we are told in Exodus 25:

"And the LORD spake unto Moses, saying…" Exodus 25:1

It was "Yahweh" who spoke these words. And yet from comparing all four passages, we realize that it was angels who possessed God's name that were speaking. The angels could be called Yahweh. God manifestation through the angels (and men as well) is found all throughout Scripture; it occurs with the angel who meets Joshua just before the people pass into Jericho (Joshua 5:13-6:1-5). It takes place with the angel who led Israel through the wilderness as a cloud and pillar of fire (Exodus 14:19 and Deuteronomy 1:32-33). As well, the Lord Jesus brings it up to the Jews when they want to stone him for calling himself the son of God (John 10:34-36; more is said about this in the following chapter of this book). We will examine one more example together, and then move on to some "mysteries" that are now understandable in the light of God manifestation. Our final example is hidden in the story of Balaam.

6 - BALAAM AND BALAK

When we think of Balaam, we think of a talking donkey, or more so, a rebuking donkey. Balaam was a diviner, a prophet who worked for hire. He was hired by Balak, the king of Moab, to curse the people of Israel. Often as we read through these chapters, it may be almost painful to see Balaam trying to edge himself around God's boundaries, and then to see God pull him back in, even using such means as a talking donkey. The story begins with Balak's servants appearing to Balaam and asking him if he will go with them and curse Israel. Balaam responds by telling them to stay the night and he will see what the LORD speaks to him.

> And he said unto them, Lodge here this night, and I will bring you word again, as the LORD shall speak unto me: and the princes of Moab abode with Balaam. And God came unto Balaam, and said, What men are these with thee? And Balaam said unto God, Balak the son of Zippor, king of Moab, hath sent unto me, saying, Behold, there is a people come out of Egypt, which covereth the face of the earth: come now, curse me them; peradventure I shall be able to overcome them, and drive them out. And God said unto Balaam, Thou shalt not go with them; thou shalt not curse the people for they are blessed.
> Numbers 22:8-12

God's response was "no." Balaam was not to go with the messengers. He could not curse these people, they were blessed, they were the people of Yahweh, those who were called by His name. Thus, Balaam sent the people home. But Balak was not willing to hear a "no" from Balaam; again he sent his messengers, and this time God appeared to Balaam and told him that he could go with them.

"And God came unto Balaam at night, and said unto him, If the men come to call thee, rise up, and go with them; but yet the word which I shall say unto thee, that shalt thou do." Numbers 22:20

He was allowed to go, yet whatever word God spoke to him, he had to speak. He was tied to speaking the words of the LORD. This will come up all throughout this story; Balak will want Balaam to say something different, because God will only allow Balaam to bless Israel rather than curse them. But, Balaam constantly has to remind Balak that he can only speak Yahweh's words. Here are some more instances in which Balaam reiterates this point:

"And Balaam said unto Balak, Lo, I am come unto thee: have I now any power at all to say any thing? <u>The word that God putteth in my mouth, that shall I speak</u>." Numbers 22:38

"And Balaam said unto Balak, Stand by thy burnt offering and I will go: peradventure the LORD will come to meet me: and <u>whatsoever he sheweth me I will tell thee.</u> And he went to an high place. And God met Balaam: and he said unto him, I have prepared seven altars, and I have offered upon every altar a bullock and a ram." Numbers 23:3-4

"And he answered and said, Must <u>I not take heed to speak that which the LORD hath put in my mouth</u>?" Numbers 23:12

"And the LORD met Balaam, <u>and put a word in his mouth</u>, and said, Go again unto Balak, and say thus." Numbers 23:16

The LORD met Balaam. The LORD spoke to Balaam and He was in control. God was putting these words in Balaam's mouth. But, as we will see, the one called "the LORD" is again an angel. By digging a little deeper, we can find some telling clues as to the angel's identity. Let us look at the time just after Balaam's donkey spoke to him—the angel of the LORD had stood in the donkey's path and then revealed himself to Balaam. He was not pleased that Balaam had left to go curse the people of Israel, but still gave him permission to go.

"And the <u>angel of the LORD</u> said unto Balaam, Go with the men: but only the word that <u>I shall speak unto thee</u>, that thou shalt speak. So Balaam went with the princes of Balak." Numbers 22:35

Think back to what we had read about Balaam and his words. He was only allowed to speak the words of Yahweh! He could only speak the words of God! Now, bring that together with what the angel had just said here. "Only the word that <u>I shall speak unto thee</u>, that thou shalt speak." The angel just told Balaam the exact same thing! Balaam could only speak the words that the angel had spoken to him. He could only speak those things that the angel put into his mouth. This angel was the one that was called "the LORD" when "the LORD" appeared to Balaam. He was the one who gave Balaam the words to say, and he spoke the words on behalf of God. He was God's representative. He was the one who had been coming to Balaam since the beginning of the story, he was the one that had originally told Balaam "you can only speak my words." This angel was a direct ambassador for God, and so when he appeared before Balaam, it was as though God had appeared. When he spoke to Balaam, he was speaking God's words.

UNLOCKED MYSTERIES

Angels show us a beautiful example of God manifestation. When we understand this, there are a number of difficult passages that begin to make sense, and there are a handful of passages that many look at as a "mystery" that are actually understandable. In the light of God manifestation, we will spend some time explaining two of these "mysteries"—how we are told that no man has ever seen God

(1 John 4:12) yet many have seen Him; and the angel's work in creation.

Throughout many of these stories and examples that we have seen, people have come face to face with God. They saw Him in front of them, they talked to Him, and they heard His instruction. It was a very real, very tangible event to them. In this section, we will be exploring what appears as a contradiction in the word of God, but truly is not. In the passages that we examined, Abraham met God in the plains of Mamre, Moses had God appear to him, and Balaam had God come before him. Meeting God, seeing Him, and having an interaction with Him is actually a common theme throughout Scripture. In fact, some individuals have this experience multiple times. Here are some additional examples:

- Abraham saw God on another occasion:

"And the LORD appeared unto Abram, and said, Unto thy seed will I give this land: and there builded he an altar unto the LORD, who appeared unto him." Genesis 12:7

- Moses, Aaron, Nadab, Abihu, and seventy of the elders of Israel saw God:

"Then went up Moses, and Aaron, Nadab, and Abihu, and seventy of the elders of Israel: and they saw the God of Israel: and there was under his feet as it were a paved work of a sapphire stone, and as it were the body of heaven in his clearness." Exodus 24:9-10

- The LORD appeared to Solomon twice:

"The LORD became angry with Solomon because his heart was turned from the LORD God of Israel, which had appeared unto him twice." 1 Kings 11:9

What a powerful thing this would be, to have the Ruler over all things appear to you and speak with you. It would have been awe-inspiring to see Him, to look at His features, to know that He knew what you were thinking. And yet, the contradiction that we find in all of this is that while telling us that many people have had God appear to them and that many people have seen the LORD, the Bible is very clear that God cannot be seen.

"Now unto the King eternal, immortal, invisible, the only wise God, be honor and glory for ever and ever. Amen." 1 Timothy 1:17

When writing to Timothy, Paul speaks of God and very clearly states that God is INVISIBLE. How then was it possible for all of those whom we read about, how was it possible for them to SEE God? When we combine these words of Paul with the testimony of John, the contradiction grows even more apparent.

"No man hath seen God at any time. If we love one another, God dwelleth in us, and his love is perfected in us." 1 John 4:12

The apostle is very straightforward. NO MAN hath seen God at any time. It has never taken place. None of us have ever seen God, none of us have ever gazed upon Him, none of us have ever looked straight at Him. Paul told us that He was invisible; someone could have possibly seen God if somehow they were given the ability to see invisible things at that moment. However, John squashes that idea by saying "No, in addition to His invisibility, no one has ever seen him. Ever." Add to this the truth that God spoke to Moses:

"And he said, Thou canst not see my face: for there shall no man see me, and live." Exodus 33:20

If somehow, we were able to see things that were invisible and so saw God, we would die. When we bring all of these words together, Paul told us that God is invisible, John says that no one has ever seen him at any time, and God says that even if we did see His face somehow, we would die! How does this fit together with the many passages that we saw earlier? Why does the Bible tell us that many have seen God and at the same time tell us that no one has seen Him? The answer lies within the realm of God manifestation.

Think back to Abraham's visit from the LORD before the destruction of Sodom and Gomorrah. Who was it that he saw? He saw three angels who were called by God's name! He saw "the LORD" because he saw the angels, but he didn't literally see Yahweh! He saw God's representatives, those who showed Yahweh beautifully! Thus, because he saw those representatives, we are told that he saw and conversed with "the LORD"! The conclusion is the same with all of these other occurrences. Scripture does not contradict itself! No one has ever seen God, He is invisible, and if they had actually seen His face, they would have died. Therefore, when the Bible tells us that people saw Yahweh, they did not literally see Him, but instead they saw an angel who represented Him and could be called by His name. They saw an "angel of His presence" (Isaiah 63:9).

Understanding God manifestation helps us to understand things that many may look at as a "great mystery," and something which cannot be known. Thankfully, when we see the Truth of the Bible, everything seems to fit. This is true as well when we look at the angel's part in creation. Often when speaking to a Trinitarian, one of the passages brought up to prove Jesus' preexistence with God is Genesis 1:26-27.

> And God said, <u>Let us make man in our image, after our likeness</u>: and let them have dominion over the fish of the sea, and over the fowl of the air, and over the cattle, and over all the earth, and over every creeping thing that creepeth upon the earth. So God created man in his own image, in the image of God created he him; male and female created he them. Genesis 1:26-27

Because God said, "Let us make man in our image," it is said that God must therefore be plural, and it is God, Jesus, and the Holy Spirit who are speaking to each other. They are the "us." This is not a solid conclusion to draw from this passage whatsoever. At best, it is tenuous. Unless the framework of the Trinity is first read into this passage, it doesn't read as such at all. Instead, it would just sound as though a group of people, who were collectively called "God," were speaking to each other.

As we seek for a solution to this mystery, remember that the word "elohim" is also used to denote the angels. Thus, the term "God" here is plural, possibly referring to God and the angels. In the account of creation in Genesis, the "let us make man..." can be the Father and the angels speaking to one another. But, let us not just leave this idea without any proof. Take a look at Job 38.

> Where wast thou when I laid the foundations of the earth? declare, if thou hast understanding. Who hath laid the measures thereof, if thou knowest? or who hath stretched the line upon it? Whereupon are the foundations thereof fastened? or who laid the corner stone thereof; when the morning stars sang together, and all the <u>sons of God</u> shouted for joy? Job 38:4-7

Near the end of the book of Job, God confronted Job and basically reminded him of his small stature before the God of the world. These verses are part of that reminder. God asked Job if he had existed all the way from the time of creation until that exact moment in time. He was showing Job His eternal nature, showing Job that He, the God of Israel HAD existed from the beginning. "Where were you when I laid the foundations of the earth?" His closing comment upon this section shows us the presence of the angels in the creation, "when the morning stars sang together, and all the sons of God shouted for joy?" The morning stars and sons of God were singing for joy during creation, when the foundation of the earth was laid. We know that this is referring to the angels. It could not have been Jesus, because "sons of God" is plural! It could not have been Adam and Eve because they were not alive at the creation of the world. Thus, "the sons of God" would have to be the angels. The angels were present at the creation, and from Genesis 1, in which "God" could apply to the angels, it sounds as though they took a prominent part in the birth of man.

As we look at the next part of the phrase in Genesis, we are told that God said "Let us make man <u>in our image,</u>

after our likeness." This is a strong point of identification with the angels because often angels have appeared as men. Again, the example of Abraham in Genesis 18 comes to mind. Hebrews 13 also reminds of us this.

"Be not forgetful to entertain strangers: for thereby some have entertained angels unawares." Hebrews 13:2

Some have entertained angels unaware because angels look like men! We were made in the likeness of the angels. In fact, when one looks at the word "likeness" it seems to indicate this exact idea—a resemblance in form. Unlike "image" which is probably more along the lines of moral image (basically our tendency toward good and evil, our moral nature), "likeness" refers to a similarity of form. Here are other examples where the word is used:

"And king Ahaz went to Damascus to meet Tiglathpileser king of Assyria, and saw an altar that was at Damascus: and king Ahaz sent to Urijah the priest the fashion of the altar, and the pattern of it, according to all the workmanship thereof." 2 Kings 16:10

"Then I beheld, and lo a likeness as the appearance of fire: from the appearance of his loins even downward, fire; and from his loins even upward, as the appearance of brightness, as the colour of amber." Ezekiel 8:2

"And, behold, one like the similitude of the sons of men touched my lips: then I opened my mouth, and spake, and said unto him that stood before me, O my lord, by the vision my sorrows are turned upon me, and I have retained no strength." Daniel 10:16

Angels and men look alike. Hence the belief that angels do <u>not</u> have wings, since men and angels look the same. We were made in the likeness of the angels! The "God" that is mentioned in Genesis 1 is referring to the angels and possibly the Father as well. We understand that the angels were present at creation through Job 38, and from Hebrews 13 we can also see that angels and men look similar. Bringing all of this together, understanding the angels in creation helps us to have a more accurate picture of the creation account in Genesis, and helps us to Biblically explain another passage which is often (without strong proof at all) used to prove the Trinity.

The angels are God's representatives and they give us a powerful picture of God manifestation in action. We have seen them called "God," we have seen them called "the LORD," and through understanding what it really means when they are referred to in that way, we can understand why the Bible tells us that no man has ever seen God and yet also says many times that people did see Him. Finally, this understanding of God manifestation helps us to see a true picture of creation, and also gives us a strong foundation upon which to see Jesus' relationship with his Father.

FOLLOWING THE ANGELS

A Summary

1. If we read of someone called "God" in Scripture that means that they are the God of Heaven. True/False

2. Just before Sodom and Gomorrah was destroyed, the _____ appeared to Abraham.

3. As we later find out, the three men who appeared to Abraham were actually angels. Give two verses that prove this:

   _____

   _____

4. How do we know that Moses saw an angel manifesting God at the burning bush?

5. Fill in the blanks: The apostle Stephen tells that an _____ gave the law (Acts _____). Exodus 20:1-2 tells us that the law was given by _____. This is an example of God manifestation with angels.

6. If no man has seen God at any time, and yet Scripture tells us that many people have actually seen God, how do we reconcile the two?

7. Multiple Choice:
   The angels were present at creation. Which verse proves this?

       a. I don't read the Bible—it isn't important anyway
       b. John 1:1
       c. 1 Kings 9:11
       d. Job 38:7
       e. Genesis 2:7

ANSWERS:

1. False
2. LORD
3. Genesis 18:20-21 and Genesis 19:1
4. Because we are told that it was an angel, v. 2, but later the angel says that Yahweh appeared to Moses, v. 16.
5. Angel; 7:38; Yahweh
6. People saw angels manifesting God
7. d.

CHAPTER 4

IN THE FOOTSTEPS OF JESUS

The angels could carry God's name. They were His ambassadors, His messengers who worked for Him, doing His bidding. This is a cornerstone to a Biblical understanding of Jesus' relationship to his Father. In an even greater way than the angels, Jesus was God manifested in the flesh.

A PROPHET LIKE UNTO MOSES

We will begin in Deuteronomy 5:22-24. The context of this selection is the 10 commandments in verses 6-21. Moses is reiterating to Israel their history, and he brings their thoughts back to the mountain—the time in which their bones shook, their hearts melted, and their fear for God was struck. The LORD, the Maker of everything around them, dwelt on the mountain and displayed His power to them. A deafening voice proclaiming His commands was heard from the mountain, and fire and smoke were pouring forth.

> These words the LORD spake unto all your assembly in the mount out of the midst of the fire, of the cloud, and of the thick darkness, with a great voice: and he added no more. And he wrote them in two

tables of stone, and delivered them unto me. And it came to pass, when ye heard the voice out of the midst of the darkness, (for the mountain did burn with fire,) that ye came near unto me, even all the heads of your tribes, and your elders; and ye said, Behold, the LORD our God hath shewed us his glory and his greatness, and we have heard his voice out of the midst of the fire: we have seen this day that God doth talk with man, and he liveth. Deuteronomy 5:22-24

The mountain was flaming, the voice was reverberating all around them, the clouds and top of the mount were hauntingly dark. This was a fearful sight. It inspired awe, reverence, and literal terror within the people. Their God, who had destroyed the most powerful empire in the world, who had opened up an ocean for them to walk through, was displaying His power to them in an awesome and fearful way. They realized that they had heard the voice of God and lived, but they did not want anymore of this chilling and weakening experience.

Now therefore why should we die? for this great fire will consume us: if we hear the voice of the LORD our God any more, then we shall die. For who is there of all flesh, that hath heard the voice of the living God speaking out of the midst of the fire, as we have, and lived? Go thou near, and hear all that the LORD our God shall say: and speak thou unto us all that the LORD our God shall speak unto thee; and we will hear it, and do it. Verses 25-27

The presence of the angel and the power of the Father upon that mountain shook the people so greatly that they pleaded with Moses to end this event. "The fire will consume us, the voice, with all of its strength and great might will kill us on its own. No one in this world has heard the voice of God and lived as we have." And so they had a plan. Moses would go up to the mount and hear the voice of God; he would hear it for them and bring the commands back to them. He was to be an intermediary. He was to be their mediator. The fire, the terrible darkness, the forceful voice of the LORD was too much—they wanted to have someone to stand between Him and them, so that they would not die. God's reaction to all of this is:

> And the LORD heard the voice of your words, when ye spake unto me; and the LORD said unto me, I have heard the voice of the words of this people, which they have spoken unto thee: <u>they have well said all that they have spoken</u>. O that there were such an heart in them, that they would fear me, and keep all my commandments always, that it might be will with them, and with their children for ever! Go say to them, Get you into your tents again. But as for thee, stand thou here by me, and I will speak unto thee all the commandments, and the statues, and the judgments, which thou shalt teach them, that they may do them in the land which I give them to possess it. Verses 28-31

Look at that! God heard the words of the people, spoke to Moses, and said "they have well said"! He said, "The people understand the fear of me, they realize my strength and power, and their idea is good. Tell them to go back to their tents. You will come up to me and bring my words to them. The people are too frail and weak to see and hear me in my glory. Thus, you come up to me and be their mediator."

It is important for us to notice here that God Himself endorsed this way of communicating with the congregation. He said "they have well said." Their plan was good. This is what HE wanted to do! He wanted Moses to be a mediator.

Keep in mind that God didn't support this plan because He had a problem and needed help. He did not need someone to mediate for Him to the people. Instead, it was the other way around. The people could not handle the glory and majesty of their God! In their sinfulness, in their weakness and fear, they could not be in the presence of God. Moses was used as a mediator for the people, because THEY needed him. Remember this incident—the request at Sinai—as we move to Deuteronomy 18.

> The LORD thy God will raise up unto thee a Prophet from the midst of thee, of thy brethren, like unto me; unto him ye shall hearken; according to all that thou desiredst of the LORD thy God in Horeb in the day of the assembly, saying, Let me not hear again the voice of the LORD my God, neither let me see this great fire any more, that I die not. And the LORD said unto me, They have well spoken that which they have spoken. I will raise them up a Prophet from among their brethren, like unto thee, and will put my words in his mouth; and he shall speak unto them all that I shall command him. Deuteronomy 18:15-18

This passage is referring to the same event as Deuteronomy 5 —when God visited the people and proclaimed the law to them. It rehearses the same story, in which God said that the words that the people had spoken were good, and He confirmed them. But, notice here that it is used in a very different context! "The LORD thy God will raise up unto thee a Prophet from the midst of thee, of thy brethren, like unto me; unto him ye shall hearken." God refers back to this incident at Horeb and doesn't just apply it to Moses, but to someone who was going to come later, to a future Prophet! He says that one would come later who would be a mediator to the people, just as Moses was. When reading through the New Testament, we find out who was the fulfillment of that prophecy. It was the Lord Jesus, according to Acts 3! God takes these words and applies them to Jesus, someone who would do the exact same thing as Moses, someone who would be a mediator to the people. He would hear the words of God and declare them to the people. He would be a representative of God and deliver His message. He would speak on behalf of God. As it says in verse 18, "He shall speak unto them all that I shall command him." And, as we will see in this study, not only would he speak the words of God, but he would go even further. This "Prophet," our Lord Jesus Christ, would be an exact representation of God. He would perfectly show God's character, God's purpose, God's actions. He would manifest God in a beautiful way.

GOD MANIFESTING HIMSELF THROUGH JESUS

Jesus is an awesome example of God manifestation. He was a perfect representation of his Father. During his ministry (and now as well) he showed who the LORD was; he never sinned, and he always did what the Father would have done. Think about what it would have been like to spend a day with him—it would have been like spending a day with God. He had the characteristics of God: those of mercy, grace, patience, kindness, fullness of truth, justice, among others. When people looked at Christ, they essentially saw the Father. Jesus tells us this in John 14:

> If ye had known me, ye should have known my Father also: and from henceforth ye know him, and have seen him. Philip saith unto him, Lord, show us the Father, and it sufficeth us. Jesus saith unto him, Have I been so long time with you, and yet hast thou not known me, Philip? <u>he that hath seen me hath seen the Father</u>; and how sayest thou then, Show us the Father? John 14:7-9

If we had been in Jerusalem, or if we had been able to watch Jesus, if we had been able to listen to him, if we had been able to sit at his feet, his actions would have been beautiful. In fact, Jesus was such a perfect representative of God, that his actions were the same actions that God would have taken if he had been there. Jesus is telling Philip that time spent with him was basically time spent with God. If he saw the things that Jesus did, he essentially saw the things that God would have done.

Often this passage is advanced by Trinitarians to prove that Jesus truly is very God of very God. They read the passage literally, and essentially make Jesus to say "Philip, I am God, just look at me." However, this interpretation also causes them to stumble. If the passage is taken literally, it doesn't just say that Jesus is God, but goes even further. This verse says that Jesus IS HIS FATHER! This can be difficult for the Trinitarian to explain, because according to their model, God the Father is NOT God the Son. The Father and the Son are both God, but the Father is not the Son. I have talked to many Trinitarians about this passage, and in one particular instance when a minister was giving me this explanation of the verses, I asked him, "How then do you explain a son who is his Father?" The reply was, "It's a mystery." This is the same limp explanation you will receive from many Trinitarians. If we take the passage literally, that is the problem that we will find—Jesus is saying that he is his Father, which is completely incomprehensible. However, by understanding the passage figuratively, we see Jesus saying that if you looked at him you would KNOW God, and would have seen the Father because he, Jesus, acted the same as the LORD would have. Spending a day with Jesus was as though you were spending a day with God. They did the exact same thing that the other would have done. Jesus acted on God's authority! Jesus carried the name of God, and his power worked within him. Christ reinforced this conclusion, telling us that the actions he did were not his own! He was doing what he had seen God do.

"Then answered Jesus and said unto them, Verily, verily, I say unto you, <u>The Son can do nothing of himself, but what he seeth the Father do: for what things soever he doeth, these also doeth the Son likewise</u>." John 5:19

The testimony here is very straightforward! Jesus said that he could not do ANYTHING by himself, but he could only do the things that his Father had shown him, or taught him. He followed the actions of his Father. To add to this, he also spoke God's words, fulfilling the prophecy that we read in Deuteronomy 18. This is shown to us time and again:

"Then said Jesus unto them, When ye have lifted up the Son of man, then shall ye know that I am he, and that <u>I do nothing of myself; but as my Father hath taught me, I speak these things</u>." John 8:28

"For I have not spoken of myself; but the Father which sent me, <u>he gave me a commandment, what I should say, and what I should speak</u>." John 12:49

"He that loveth me not keepeth not my sayings: and <u>the word which ye hear is not mine, but the Father's which sent me</u>." John 14:24

The Lord was speaking the words of his Father. He was acting the actions of his Father. He was a perfect ambassador, perfect representative of God. Seeing Jesus and speaking to Jesus were as though you were seeing God and speaking to God. Not only does Jesus himself tell us these things, the writer to the Hebrews says the same:

"God, who at sundry times and in divers manners spake in time past unto the fathers by the prophets, hath in these last days <u>spoken unto us by his Son</u>, whom he hath appointed heir of all things, by whom also he made the worlds." Hebrews 1:1-2

In the past, before the days of Christ, God had spoken to us through the prophets. But now, He has a new way. In these days, He speaks to us through Jesus. Jesus' words were God's words. He was not speaking of his own, but rather as a representative working on behalf of God. He was working solely for the glory, praise, and honor of his Father. He was seeking to bring exaltation to the name of God which he carried. He was dependent upon God for righteous words and actions, and God taught him who he should be.

Jesus' actions were God's actions. Jesus' words were God's words. He was not literally the Father, but rather he showed the same character as God. As it said in John 5, "for whatever the Father does, that the Son does likewise."

THE IMAGE OF GOD

A mirror is an excellent example of Jesus' relationship with his Father. I have a mirror in my bathroom; when I get up in the morning and start to get ready for the day, I can look at myself and watch myself brush my teeth and wash my face. However, what I see isn't actually me. When I look into a mirror—when you look into a mirror—we do not actually see ourselves, but we see an image of ourselves. This image does what we do. When I move my arm, the image's arm moves as well! When I smile, the image smiles back at me. When you look into a mirror, you see an image of yourself, which does the same things as you. Based off of this, you could even say that he who has seen you in the mirror, has seen you. Does that sound familiar?

In Scripture, Jesus is actually referred to as the image of God. He is God's image. The two share the same character and do the same things, but they are not one being! Jesus was God being manifested in the flesh. As Paul said to the Corinthians:

"In whom the god of this world hath blinded the minds of them which believe not, lest the light of the glorious gospel of Christ, who is the image of God, should shine unto them." 2 Corinthians 4:4

These verses in Corinthians speak of Jesus as God's image! They tell us that Jesus wasn't the same as the Father, but he was a perfect image of Him, and that he possessed God's complete character. If Jesus possessed God's image, when one looked at him, as we saw in John 14, it was as though they were looking at God. He could say, "He that has seen me has seen the Father." Jesus followed God's actions exactly and was the greatest example of God's name—mercy, grace, longsuffering, goodness, truth, and justice—that we have ever seen.

DECLARING GOD'S NAME

And in fact, this was something that Christ had set out to do. He was sent to this world to show Israel, and eventually the world, God's character. He was sent to bear his Father's name, to act as God would act, to speak God's words. In his final prayer with his disciples before his crucifixion, Jesus prayed:

"I have manifested thy name unto the men which thou gavest me out of the world: thine they were, and thou gavest them me; and they have kept thy word." John 17:6

In this way, though no one had ever seen God before, they could know Him though His son. They could see God as they gazed upon His "image." They could know Him through the actions and words of Jesus.

"No man hath seen God at any time, the only begotten Son, which is in the bosom of the Father, he hath declared him." John 1:18

Through Jesus, people could know the Father. They could observe and see the way that Jesus treated the poor of God's people and they could understand how God felt about the destitute. They could watch Jesus interact with the Pharisees and could understand how God felt about apostasy and those who left His truth for a lie. God manifestation is a powerful way in which we can learn about the character of God. We can see God's mercy as we watch Jesus reach down and touch the leprous man and make him whole (Matthew 8). We can see God's longsuffering as we watch Jesus continue to work with Peter, even after his denial (John 21). We can see God's justice as we watch Jesus condemn the religious leaders for their hypocrisy and lack of knowledge (Luke 11). Jesus came to declare his Father through the things that he did and said. He made his Father known to the world. Because we understand this, because we see Jesus as a perfect manifestation of the Father, then the passages which refer to Christ as "God" or "the LORD" fit perfectly. If the angels were called "the LORD" or "God" because they were God's ambassadors, even more could Christ be called the same. He was a flawless and gracious manifestation. Let's actually take a look at some of these passages.

"For unto us a child is born, unto us a son is given: and the government shall be upon his shoulder: and his name shall be called Wonderful, Counsellor, The mighty God, The everlasting Father, The Prince of Peace." Isaiah 9:6

Referring to the second coming of Christ, we are told that "the LORD my God shall come":

"And ye shall flee to the valley of the mountains; for the valley of the mountains shall reach unto Azal: yea, ye shall flee, like as ye fled from before the earthquake in the days of Uzziah king of Judah: and the LORD my God shall come, and all the saints with thee." Zechariah 14:5

Thomas also speaks of Christ in this way:

And after eight days again his disciples were within, and Thomas with them: then came Jesus, the doors being shut, and stood in the midst, and said, Peace be unto you. Then saith he to Thomas, Reach hither thy finger, and behold my hands; and reach hither thy hand, and thrust it into my side: and be not faithless, but believing. And Thomas answered and said unto him, My Lord and my God. John 20:26-28

After Christ's resurrection, Thomas finally understood Jesus' connection to his Father. Thomas understood that Jesus was a representative of God, and understood that he was God's son, thus his exclamation "my Lord and my God."

JESUS AND THE TRINITY

This view of Jesus is very different than the fictitious view of the Trinity. The teaching of the Trinity says that there is one God, yet the Father is God and Jesus is God and the Holy Spirit is also God. However, there are not three Gods, but still only one. In addition, it also puts forth that Jesus and the Father were one being, but also separate and distinct. Trying to truly grasp how three beings can all be God, but the existence of only one God, is an impossible feat and helps you to understand why so many Trinitarians just say "it's a mystery." The dogma of the Trinity is completely and utterly incomprehensible. However, in the light of Scripture, and what we have talked about with God manifestation, let us compare the two views and see which stand up to our scrutiny.

The two viewpoints are—

1. *Jesus was one being with the Father, being 100% man and 100% God at the same time (Trinity).*
2. *Jesus was a representative of God, perfectly manifesting His character and power. Jesus' thoughts were God's thoughts (God manifestation).*

When we start to compare these beliefs to Scripture, immediately we run into contradictions created by the Trinity. The first of these is the fact that God cannot die. If Jesus were God, it would have been impossible for him to have ever died on the cross. In 1 Timothy 1, the apostle writes about God's immortality. God cannot die!

"Now unto the King eternal, <u>immortal</u>, invisible, the only wise God, be honor and glory for ever and ever. Amen." 1 Timothy 1:17

God is immortal. And yet we know that Jesus died; this is a plain truth of the gospel:

"For I delivered unto you first of all that which I also received, how that <u>Christ died</u> for our sins according to the scriptures; and that he was buried, and that he rose again the third day according to the scriptures." 1 Corinthians 15:3-4

God cannot die, and yet Jesus was crucified and killed on the cross. Some Trinitarians have tried to answer this contradiction by reminding us that (according to their belief) Jesus was 100% man and also 100% God; thus, when he was crucified, the portion of him that was man died and the God portion stayed alive. However, God's Word NEVER says anything to this end. There is not a single verse that refers to Jesus as a "God-man" or that says anything about him being totally God and totally man at the same time. This idea is devoid of any Scriptural truth. Thankfully, when we see Jesus in the truth of God manifestation, this contradiction completely vanishes.

Another problem that is created by the belief of the Trinity begins with the fact that Jesus was tempted to sin. Hebrews 4 tells us that Jesus was tempted "in every point...as we are." He knows what it feels like to want to do something wrong. For this reason, he can empathize with us and understand what we are going through when we struggle with sin.

"For we have not an high priest which cannot be touched with the feeling of our infirmities; but was in all points tempted like as we are, yet without sin." Hebrews 4:15

Because he was human, he wanted to do things that would have been wrong, despite his love for God. Through his Father's strength, he was able to defeat those urges. This is an important point for us to realize. If it were impossible for Christ to be tempted by sin, then all of his temptations in the wilderness would have been pointless. It is not possible for something to be a temptation if we don't want to do it. Let me give you an example. I really love steak. I enjoy eating it for dinner, I would enjoy eating it for lunch, and I've even had it for breakfast and liked it. Contrast this to a vegetarian, who would not want to eat steak at all. Now, imagine that a vegetarian and I were sitting together at a table. Two steaks were set in front of us and we were told that it had just become a sin to eat steak. For me, I would still be tempted to eat the steak, even though I knew that it was wrong. I would be tempted because I like steak. On the other hand, the vegetarian wouldn't even give the steak a second thought.

They wouldn't care that there was red meat in front of them, and they would not be tempted at all. Steak isn't something that they would want to eat, and so there is no temptation for them. In order for a temptation to occur, you have to have a desire for that temptation! Jesus must have wanted to do things that were wrong at times in his life. This is not to say that he ever did them. He was perfect and flawless (1 Peter 2:22)—but still had a human nature. This is powerful point because it shows that there were times when Christ wanted to do what he should not (he loved God with all of his being, but his humanity still pulled at him) and yet, he never gave in to it.

Jesus was tempted. Yet the contradiction created by the Trinity appears when we read that God "cannot be tempted with evil." God hates sin, He totally despises it, and it is so completely against His nature, that He is never tempted to do so. James chapter 1 puts it very plainly:

"Let no man say when he is tempted, I am tempted of God: for <u>God cannot be tempted with evil</u>, neither tempteth he any man." James 1:13

On top of these two contradictions, there are many others. The chart on the back of this page gives a list of ten contradictions (including the two that we examined in detail) that arise when one believes the doctrine of the Trinity.

10 CONTRADICTIONS IF JESUS WERE LITERALLY GOD

Jesus	God
1. Jesus died: - 1 Corinthians 15:3-4	1. God cannot die: - 1 Timothy 1:17
2. Jesus was tempted: - Hebrews 4:15	2. God cannot be tempted: - James 1:13
3. Jesus was seen: - John 1:29	3. No man has ever seen God: - 1 John 4:12
4. Jesus was and is a man: - 1 Timothy 2:5	4. God is not a man: - Numbers 23:19
5. Jesus had to grow and learn: - Hebrews 5:8-9	5. God does not ever need to learn: - Isaiah 40:28
6. Jesus needed salvation: - Hebrews 5:7	6. God does not: - Hebrews 5:7
7. Jesus grew weary: - John 4:6	7. God cannot grow weary: - Isaiah 40:28
8. Jesus slept: - Matthew 8:24	8. God does not slumber: - Psalm 121:2-4
9. Jesus was not omnipotent: - John 5:19	9. God's power is not limited: - Isaiah 45:5-7
10. Jesus did not know everything: - Mark 13:32	10. There is nothing that God does not know: - Isaiah 46:10

JESUS WORSHIPPED THE FATHER

These 10 contradictions form quite a barrier to a Scriptural belief in the Trinity. The verses are totally incompatible with the doctrine. As we saw in chapter 1, just dismissing the contradictions as a mystery is not acceptable. These contradictions call for answers but none arise. When we leaf through Scripture to search for answers, we learn more about the relationship between God and Jesus which is incompatible with the doctrine of the Trinity, but fits wonderfully with God manifestation. Time and time again, the Father is called Jesus' "God," and Jesus worshipped the Father.

"Jesus saith unto her, Touch me not; for I am not yet ascended to my Father: but go to my brethren, and say unto them, I ascend unto my Father, and your Father; and to <u>my God</u>, and your God." John 20:17

"The <u>God and Father of our Lord Jesus Christ</u>, which is blessed for evermore, knoweth that I lie not." 2 Corinthians 11:31

"Wherefore I also, after I heard of your faith in the Lord Jesus, and love unto all the saints, cease not to give thanks for you, making mention of you in my prayers; that <u>the God of our Lord Jesus Christ</u>, the Father of glory, may give unto you the spirit of wisdom and revelation in the knowledge of him." Ephesians 1:15-17

"Blessed be <u>the God and Father of our Lord Jesus Christ</u>, which according to his abundant mercy hath begotten us again unto a lively hope by the resurrection of Jesus Christ from the dead." 1 Peter 1:3

"Him that overcometh will I make a pillar in the temple of my God, and he shall go no more out: and I will write upon him the name of my God, and the name of the city of my God, which is new Jerusalem, which cometh down out of heaven from my God: and I will write upon him my new name." Revelation 3:12

The strongest of all of these references is Revelation 3. Not only is God called Christ's God, but He is called that four times in a single verse! Through these verses we understand more of the relationship between Jesus and his Father. His Father was his God. Jesus worshipped and followed his Father. His Father was and is the supreme being of the universe and Jesus was and is His son.

SENT AND GIVEN AUTHORITY BY HIS FATHER

Since God is the ruler of all creation, then it follows that Jesus would be given all of the things that he has from his Father and that his Father would have more authority than him. This is indeed what we see taught in Scripture, again incompatible with the doctrine of the Trinity, but harmonizing perfectly with God manifestation.

"And he saith unto them, Ye shall drink indeed of my cup, and be baptized with the baptism that I am baptized with: but to sit on my right hand, and on my left, is not mine to give, but it shall be given to them for whom it is prepared of my Father." Matthew 20:23

Jesus did not have the authority to give the seats on his right and left sides, but his Father did.

"And Jesus came and spake unto them, saying, All power <u>is given unto me</u> in heaven and in earth." Matthew 28:18

Jesus was GIVEN all power in heaven and earth, it was not something that was innate within him, but something he was given. And who gave it to him? His Father!

"For I have not spoken of myself; but <u>the Father which sent me, he gave me a commandment</u>, what I should say, and what I should speak." John 12:49

He was sent by God. God gave him a command and he followed it. Note the One who wielded sovereignty.

"Jesus knowing that <u>the Father had given all things into his hands</u>, and that he was come from God, and went to God..." John 13:3

All things were given into his hands FROM HIS FATHER.

"Father, I will that they also, whom <u>thou hast given me</u>, be with me where I am; that they may behold <u>my glory, which thou hast given me</u>: for thou lovedst me before the foundation of the world." John 17:24

Who gave Jesus his glory? HIS FATHER!

"The God of Abraham, and of Isaac, and of Jacob, the <u>God of our fathers, hath glorified his Son Jesus</u>; whom ye delivered up, and denied him in the presence of Pilate, when he was determined to let him go." Acts 3:13

It was God who glorified Jesus. God was the one who lifted him up from the grave and gave him power and a throne.

"The God of our fathers raised up Jesus, whom ye slew and hanged on a tree. Him hath <u>God exalted with his right hand</u> to be a Prince and a Savior, for to give repentance to Israel, and forgiveness of sins." Acts 5:30-31

This verse tells us the same as the previous one. God was the one who exalted Jesus.

"The Revelation of Jesus Christ, <u>which God gave unto him</u>, to shew unto his servants things which must shortly come to pass; and he sent and signified it by his angel unto his servant John." Revelation 1:1

Finally, even after his exaltation to glory, God GAVE the Revelation to Jesus. There is a clear line of authority. God is in command and has given His power and glory to His son. This is not said in any way to diminish the might and majesty of Christ, who will have all nations bow before him (Philippians 2:10-11). But it is said to help us see the true teaching of Scripture—that the Father is the omnipotent and everlasting God, and He gave these qualities to Jesus. Unlike the Trinity, which teaches that Jesus and God are co-equal, the Scriptures teach a direct hierarchy.

COEQUAL?

God is the clear source of power and authority in this universe and there is not a co-equal relationship between God and Jesus.

"Ye have heard how I said unto you, I go away, and come again unto you. If ye loved me, ye would rejoice, because I

said, I go unto the Father: for <u>my Father is greater than I</u>."
John 14:28

Jesus states "my Father is greater than I." His words are
simple, God is greater than he is. In no way can this mean
equality. God is the supreme ruler. He has given His rulership
to His son, who will eventually give it back to Him. Many
Trinitarians try to explain this verse by saying that it was
spoken while Jesus was on earth, while he was "God in the
flesh" and since he was in flesh, he was inferior to his Father.
This is not a legitimate explanation. After Jesus' exaltation to
glory and honor, another statement about him and his
Father's equality is made:

"And when all things shall be subdued unto him, <u>then shall
the Son also himself be subject unto him that put all things
under him</u>, that God may be all in all." 1 Corinthians 15:28

Even after being raised up, even after being given the power
of God, Christ will still be subject to God, that GOD may be
all in all. The Father is the source of authority, the Father is
the sovereign ruler, and the Father is the One who has given
all power to His son.

By seeing the Truth of Scripture, we don't have to
dismiss these contradictions and problems with the Trinity by
saying that they are "part of a mystery," and building up our
salvation upon a crumbling tower of confusion. We can piece
together the Scriptures and understand Jesus as he really is!
We can see him as a man (Hebrews 2:14 and 17), the son of
God. He was perfect, never sinning (Hebrews 4:15) and was
given the power and authority of his Father (John 17:2). He
was God's greatest representative. Now all of the
contradictions are answered.

Jesus is called God because he represented Him. He was the best representative of God to have ever lived. His representation of his Father was flawless, it was perfect. Through looking at his character, people saw God's character. As we discussed earlier, Jesus was the image of God. Those things that God did, Jesus did as well. Jesus was God being manifested, or revealed, in the flesh. This is why Jesus said that he and his Father were one (John 10:30). They were completely one in mind, one in purpose, and one in character.

"I AND MY FATHER ARE ONE"

When Christ said "I and my Father are one," he didn't mean that they were one body or one person; rather, he meant that they were one in character. If I were to say that my best friend and I were one, you would not think that I was saying that we were one person, but you would understand that we thought in the same way, we did everything together. When Jesus said that he and God were "one," he was NOT saying that they were one person. Instead, he was speaking of a "oneness" relationship that is very similar to the relationship between a husband and a wife. The way that the Father and His son are "one" is very similar to the way that a man and woman become one, but even more intimate. Here is what Jesus says about marriage:

"And said, For this cause shall a man leave father and mother, and shall cleave to his wife: and they twain shall be one flesh? Wherefore they are no more twain, but <u>one flesh</u>. What therefore God hath joined together, let not man put asunder." Matthew 19:5-6

Jesus says that a husband and a wife are "one flesh" (quoting from Genesis 2). He then goes on to say that the husband and wife, who once were two people, are now one. The question to ask becomes, "How are they one?"

We know either from our own wedding or from attending others' weddings, that the people who were just married did not suddenly become one being. Their bodies did not suddenly fuse together as soon as the words "I now pronounce you husband and wife" were uttered. Rather, their marriage bound them together in a special bond. It was a bond saying that they would strive to act as one being. It did not mean that the bride would go to work with the groom and never leave his side, but that they would hold the same goals, they would have the same mind, the same values.

Unfortunately, when Christ said to the Jews that he was one with his Father, they misunderstood him and became angry. They believed that he was saying that he was God, that he was saying that he and the Father were the same person, and so they wanted to stone him. Jesus went on to explain to them what he was saying—and his explanation is amazing. Starting at verse 29,

> My Father, which gave them me, is greater than all; and no man is able to pluck them out of my Father's hand. I and my Father are one. Then the Jews took up stones again to stone him. Jesus answered them, Many good works have I shewed you from my Father; for which of those works do ye stone me? The Jews answered him, saying, For a good work we stone thee not; but for blasphemy; and because that thou, being a man, makest thyself God. Jesus answered them, Is it not written in your law, I said, Ye are gods? <u>If he called them gods,</u>

<u>unto whom the word of God came, and the scripture cannot be broken; say ye of him, whom the Father hath sanctified, and sent into the world, Thou blasphemest; because I said, I am the Son of God?</u> John 10:29-30

He and his Father were one. Just like a husband and a wife, they were one of mind and one of purpose. This was the epicenter of what Jesus was saying. He was trying to get the Jews to understand this about him, that he was a representative of God. Instead, they picked up stones to stone him because they thought that he was making himself God. His answer was: "Stop. Isn't it written in your own law 'I said, ye are gods'?" Jesus took the Jews' minds back to Psalm 82:6. He brought their minds back to God manifestation. He showed them that the Old Testament addressed their leaders as "gods." That word in Psalm 82 is "elohim." The Jewish leaders were called "God" because they held His authority with the people and were supposed to make godly decisions. They were His ambassadors. Christ's point is, if the Jewish leaders were called "gods," then would it not be appropriate for Jesus himself, the one whom the Father had sanctified and sent into the world, to say that he was God? But in fact, he then steps back from that argument and says "there would have been nothing wrong had I called myself 'God,' but that's not even what I did. I said I was His son." Jesus was one with his Father. They were one in character and purpose.

We have looked at Jesus' relationship to his Father. Jesus was the son of God and could be called "God." When people looked at Jesus, essentially they saw the Father—not because they looked the same, but because they acted the same way. Jesus was like a mirror image of God; he performed the same actions that God would have performed if He had been there. When trying to understand God and

Christ's relationship in the light of the Trinity, many contradictions arise. However, these contradictions disappear when we view Jesus as a representative, instead of God himself. Not only did he represent his Father, but he also was one with Him. They were one in spirit, in the same way that a husband and wife are one flesh.

IN THE FOOTSTEPS OF JESUS

A Summary

1. Moses was a mediator between God and the people. What chapter and verses told that another would come after him who did the same type of thing?

2. Multiple Choice:
   Jesus said "He that hath seen me hath seen the Father." What does that mean?
   a. That Jesus is his Father
   b. That Jesus did the actions and spoke the words of God
   c. That Jesus and God look physically identical
   d. It's a mystery

3. Constantly Scripture tells us that Jesus spoke God's words. List three verses that say this.

   _____   _____
   _____

4. 2 Corinthians 4:4 describes Jesus as the _____ of God.

5. When we piece together the testimony of all of these verses, we learn the Truth about Christ. Who was he?

6. The Trinity often contradicts the Bible. What are two of these contradictions?
   - _____
   - _____

7. Fill in the blank: We are often told that the LORD was Jesus' God. Revelation _____ tells us this and so does 2 Corinthians _____.

8. Jesus and God have equal status. True/False

9. Multiple Choice:

> Jesus was and is one with his Father. This means:
>
>> a. That Jesus and God shared the same goals, the same character
>>
>> b. That they were not two
>>
>> c. That they were one substance
>>
>> d. That they existed together from the beginning

ANSWERS:

1. Deuteronomy 18:18
2. b.
3. Any of the verses on pgs. 73-74
4. Image
5. He was God's son, a perfect representative of His Father
6. Any of the contradictions from the chart on pg. 82
7. 3:12; 11:31
8. False
9. a.

CHAPTER 5

UNITED WITH CHRIST

T he scope of God manifestation has brought us to see the angels as God's representatives, and encouraged us to see Jesus as the mirror image of God, the one who followed and worked for his God perfectly. It has greatly helped us to understand our Father—in him we can see God's actions, we can see God's longsuffering, His lovingkindness, and His faithfulness. By grasping these truths, so many of the things that used to be "mysteries" have been revealed. God has revealed them all in Scripture, we just have to look for them. As we continue on our journey through the Word, we will see how God manifestation impacts our hope—the crown of glory which we seek to be given. We will see how we can be united with Christ. We will speak of Jesus' exaltation to glory, show how we can follow his same path of honor, and then compare this hope to the Marriage of the Lamb.

POSSESSING THE NAME OF GOD

As we mentioned earlier, there is a slight difference between being "called by" God's name, and actually "possessing" that name (chapter 2, page 31). Let me give an example to illustrate: let's imagine that you were driving to work today, and it had been a great morning. You were listening to your favorite song, the sky was beautiful, and you were feeling joyful about the life that God had given to you. Your thoughts were drifting, you were thinking about thankfulness, and thinking about the beauty of the sky in front of you. Regrettably, because your mind was so occupied with your thoughts, you weren't paying attention as you were merging onto the freeway. You began to move into the lane, and then suddenly someone was violently honking their horn at you. Oops. You had accidentally cut someone off. As they drove by, you saw that they gave you "the look," and yelled "jerk!"

Let's step back from the scenario. Are you actually a jerk? Maybe you had acted in the way that a jerk would act, but that doesn't mean that you truly are one. Just because you were called such, doesn't have to mean that you don't care about the feelings and needs of others. What you had done was an accident! You were just called a jerk, but you aren't actually one. But, being called by that name still got you associated with it. Now, the person that got angry at you might see you later on that day at the bank and think "hey, it's that jerk who cut me off!" Or, they still may remember you as they eat dinner, talking to their family about the jerk that almost killed them as they were driving to work.

This is also true for a positive name. If we were helping an old lady cross the street and she called us a "helpful person," that doesn't have to mean that we are actually helpful at heart, but that we DID something that was helpful. Being called by a name just means that you have done something to associate yourself with that name, but it doesn't mean that you actually are that way all of the time.

And so it is with the name of God. When we become called by God's name, that doesn't mean that we are God, or that we have His characteristics. Just as though we aren't actually a jerk when are called one, we aren't actually God, or we may not actually be loving or merciful when we are called by His name. It just means that we represent Him and that we are associated with Him. We did something to be called by that name. We cut someone off to be called a jerk. We helped an old lady walk across the street to be called helpful. We can be baptized into Christ to be called by God's name and become associated with God. We become people who represent the Father, people who represent the Lord of the universe to those around us.

Possessing a name is very different. When you possess a name, when you possess a character, that name is who you are. If you actually were a jerk, then you would be mean and nasty almost <u>all of the time</u>! You would merge onto the freeway, see that someone was coming, slow down purposefully, and then cut them off, laughing hysterically. If that were your character, then you would possess the title of "jerk." It would be who you were. If you actually were a helpful person, that would mean that you enjoy helping people and it is something that you do often. You would possess that name; it would be part of your being.

In the same way, if you possess the name of God, then the name of God is who you are. You would be merciful, gracious, truthful, longsuffering, good, just. You would have His authority. You would be all of these things. There has only been one man that has ever possessed this name. He is the Lord Jesus Christ. After his resurrection, his Father changed his name. With that name came privileges; he was given God's power and his nature was changed; he was made immortal and the temptation to sin disappeared. The name of God was his new name.

GIVEN HIS FATHER'S NAME

Jesus did not always possess God's name. Just as we do, he began by being called by God's name. He was associated with God in the beginning, and it was not until later that he was given His glorious name.

"I am come in my Father's name, and ye receive me not: if another shall come in his own name, him ye will receive." John 5:43

Jesus came on behalf of God; he came as a representative of Him. He was associated with his Father. As time went on, things changed. Eventually, the name of the Father was given to him.

> And being found in fashion as a man, he humbled himself, and became obedient unto death, even the death of the cross. Wherefore God also hath highly exalted him, <u>and given him a name which is above every name</u>: that at the name of Jesus every knee should bow, of things in heaven, and things in earth, and things under the earth; and that every tongue should confess that Jesus Christ is Lord, to the glory of God the Father. Philippians 2:8-11

Because Christ was obedient throughout his life, because he was crucified according to the will of his Father, God exalted him and gave him a name higher than any other name. This took place after his death! He became obedient unto death, "wherefore God also hath highly exalted him." Because of his obedience, even his death on the cross, God exalted him and gave him a name which is above every name. After Jesus died, he was given God's name.

This is solidified as we move along in the passage. "So that at the name of Jesus every knee should bow." Jesus was given the name which is above every name—he was given the name of God. Christ's name was changed so that his name now stood for God's name. Thus, when someone would say "Jesus," it stood for an immortal being which had "all power in heaven and in earth (Matthew 28:18). Jesus himself also taught this same concept, that he was given God's name, in the Great Commission.

"Go ye therefore, and teach all nations, baptizing them in the name of the Father, and of the Son, and of the Holy Spirit." Matthew 28:19

Jesus told his disciples to baptize his followers IN THE NAME of the Father, and of the Son, and of the Holy Spirit. He did not say "in the names," as plural, but singular, "in the name of the Father, and of the Son, and of the Holy Spirit." When the followers of Jesus were baptized, they were not taking on three different names, but rather, just one. Jesus and God have the same name. Jesus was given the name that is above every name. Basically, the meaning behind his name was changed. Rather than "Jesus" referring to a man who was mortal, who perfectly represented God's character and never sinned, his name now refers to a man who is an immortal king. It refers to one who has "all power in heaven and in earth" (Matthew 28:18). It refers to one who would never again feel the temptation to sin. His new name, his new character, was that character of the Father. Jesus is now perfect, flawless.

Jesus was called by the name of his Father. Eventually, once made immortal, he possessed that name and perfect character and nature. The same can be so with us. We can follow the same path to glory as our Messiah. We can be called by God's name. We can be given immortality. And we too can possess God's name as our own.

THE PATH TO GLORY

As we look through this study, one of the things that may powerfully stand out to us is that Jesus' experiences are very similar to that which we can experience. He was called by the name of God. He was raised up from the dead and given immortality. After that, he was actually given that name of God as his own. What we see is that what happened to Christ is an amazing parallel to what will happen to us, through faith and the grace of God. We can be called by God's name now. We can be resurrected from the dead, made immortal, and then given the name of God as our own! This is our hope! Manifesting God is not something that is just for the angels and Christ, but it is for us as well!

> But one in a certain place testified, saying, What is man, that thou art mindful of him? or the son of man, that thou visitest him? Thou madest him a little lower than the angels; thou crownedst him with glory and honor, and didst set him over the works of thy hands: thou hast put all things in subjection under his feet. For in that he put all in subjection under him, he left nothing that is not put under him. Hebrews 2:6-8

The beginning of the letter to the Hebrews is focused mainly on proving the absolute authority of Christ over the angels. In chapter 1, the writer puts forth the proof that none of the angels have ever been called the "Son of God." He later shows that the angels were ministers to those who are called, and yet the son was actually the ruler of all things. Then, in order to advance the point of verse 5, that the angels are not the rulers of all things, he draws a quote from Psalm 8. "But one in a certain place testified, saying…" Let us observe his quote: "What is man, that thou art mindful of him? or the son of man, that thou visitest him? Thou madest him a little lower than the angels; thou crownedst him with glory and honor, and didst set him over the works of thy hands: thou hast put all things in subjection under his feet."

This psalm focuses in on man and looks at God's relation to him. "We are dust, what are we that God would even care to look upon us?" Then, in the way that many people may understand this quote, the Psalmist speaks more about creation and the hope of man. He says that in status, mankind was made a little lower than the angels. The angels had immortality. They perfectly followed the will of God. But, man was crowned with glory and honor, and all things are subject to him. He is the ruler over all, with the earth acknowledging him as king. At least, that is one way that many could read the psalm. However, the writer to the Hebrews gives us a very different interpretation.

"But now we see not yet all things put under him." Hebrews 2:8

This verse gives us an entirely new way to look at the quote from Psalm 8. The writer is saying, "Take a look at Psalm 8. Man has been made lower than the angels. BUT, he has NOT YET been given the glory. He has not yet been given the honor. Everything in this world is not yet subject to him." That is our hope. That is the hope of mankind, that they will be crowned with glory and honor, that they will rule in the Kingdom of the Father. Right now, we are just lower than the angels and nothing more. But we have a hope of greater things. The writer goes on to explain even further:

> But we see Jesus, <u>who was made a little lower than the angels</u> for the suffering of death, <u>crowned with glory and honor;</u> that he by the grace of God should taste death for every man. For it became him, for whom are all things, and by whom are all things, in bringing many sons unto glory, to make the captain of their salvation perfect through sufferings. Hebrews 2:9-10

We see Jesus as a picture of Psalm 8 in action. He was made a little lower than the angels. And now, he IS crowned with glory and honor. And soon, ALL THINGS will be in subjection to him (Psalm 110:1). Psalm 8 speaks of these things in reference to mankind, who can fulfill them in the Kingdom as part of their hope. The writer to the Hebrews shows how Jesus has already begun to work through this pattern. He ALREADY is crowned with glory and honor. Christ is our example. We are following the same process of salvation and exaltation that he went through. We are made a little lower than the angels, we can be crowned with glory and honor, and all things can be in subjection to us. He walked the same path to glory that we can walk.

CALLED BY THE NAME OF GOD

When we look at Jesus' life on earth and see that he was called by the name of God, resurrected to immortality, and given the name of God afterwards, we can look at that as the pathway which we will take throughout our journey to eternity. Let's take a look.

Jesus was called by the name of God, and in this life, we can be called by that name as well. We can associate ourselves with the glorious God! We can become His representatives. As Israel dedicated themselves to God and became a people called by His name (Deuteronomy 28:10), we can become the same, as James noted in his address to the apostles in Jerusalem:

"And after they had held their peace, James answered, saying, Men and brethren, hearken unto me: Simeon hath declared how God at the first did visit the Gentiles, to take out of them a people for his name." Acts 15:13-14

God had just opened up the way for the Gentiles (non-Jews) to hear the gospel, to hear the good news about Christ and the Kingdom! He began to call throughout the Gentiles to find people there who would accept His Truth, who would be baptized, and enter into that name. He was looking for a people for His name, people who would one day take on that name as their own. Jesus references this same idea. When we are baptized, we are bringing ourselves into the name of God:

"Go ye therefore, and teach all nations, baptizing them in the name of the Father, and of the Son, and of the Holy Ghost." Matthew 28:19

We can come into the name of God! At baptism we associate ourselves with it, we enter into it, we become people who bear that name. We are changed into God's representatives. We work on His behalf, we can speak His words. Following along the lines of this teaching, Paul tells us in Galatians that when we are baptized, we are putting on Christ!

"For as many of you as have been baptized into Christ <u>have put on Christ</u>." Galatians 3:27

Baptism, this putting on of Christ, once again, is a way of associating ourselves with Jesus. If you have put on Christ as a covering, you represent him in the things that you do. Baptism is the way that God has laid out for us to be called by His name, it is the way that God has given to allow us to be His ambassadors. Note though that this is speaking about TRUE baptism, baptism into the Truth, not baptism into a church that believes and teaches lies such as the Trinity. Only a baptism into the true Jesus is valid. By being baptized into the true Christ, the true Father, and the true Holy Spirit, we can be representatives of God.

Just as the angels were, and just as Christ was during his earthly ministry, we can be called by the name of God. By taking up our cross and being buried through the water (Romans 6:4), we can be a people for God's name. This is the point that we can reach in this life, we can become representatives of God through our baptisms. We can become people who bear His name. After that, it is then our duty to manifest God, to show others who He is by what we do. It becomes our job and our responsibility to declare God's character by the way we act, just as Jesus did while he was on the earth.

Eventually, we can even be given that name as our own. Imagine that. The actual name of God, with its power, its values, and its traits can someday be your name. The sin within you will be destroyed. All your thoughts will be glorious, beautiful, honoring thoughts. Everything you do will bring a smile to the face of the Father. But before this can all take place, there is an essential step that needs to occur.

THE FIRSTBORN FROM THE DEAD

Before he was given God's name, Jesus was raised. This is the hope that we can all share—a resurrection from the dead. We hope for a resurrection just as that of Jesus, a resurrection to immortality, a resurrection to life. And even if we have not yet died when Christ returns, all of us will be changed. Our flesh will be destroyed, and we will become spirit. In this step, a resurrection to immortality and change of nature, we too are following the same path as Christ. We may recall that often he is called the "firstborn from the dead." Paul, when speaking before King Agrippa and Festus spoke of the resurrection of Jesus:

"That Christ should suffer, and that he should be <u>the first that should rise from the dead</u>, and should shew light unto the people, and to the Gentiles." Acts 26:23

When writing to the Colossians he said the same thing:

"And he is the head of the body, the church: who is the beginning, <u>the firstborn from the dead</u>; that in all things he might have the preeminence." Colossians 1:18

As well, the apostle John wrote of Christ in this way in his introduction to the Apocalypse:

"And from Jesus Christ, who is the faithful witness, and <u>the first begotten of the dead</u>, and the prince of the kings of the earth. Unto him that loved us, and washed us from our sins in his own blood." Revelation 1:5

Implicit within this phrase of "firstborn from the dead" is the fact that others will come after. Calling Jesus the "first" means that there WILL be more. There will be a second, and a third, and so on. He is the first of many; there will be others to rise from this dead. This fits perfectly with the concept that Jesus walked the same path to glory as us. He was called by God's name, and we can be as well. He was resurrected, many of will experience a revival from the sleep of death. Jesus' resurrection is intimately connected with our resurrection. The process that he went through to receive the name of God is tied to our process. He went through the same steps that we will go through. The connection between our resurrection and his is so strong that the apostle Paul even refers to Christ's resurrection as the SAME resurrection as ours! He doesn't speak of Jesus' resurrection as a separate occurrence from ours, but actually speaks of them as the same event. Jesus began "the resurrection" when he was raised from the dead and we continue it at ours. This is Paul's line of reasoning:

> Now if Christ be preached that he rose from the dead, how say some among you that there is no resurrection of the dead? <u>But if there be no resurrection of the dead, then is Christ not risen</u>... But now is Christ risen from the dead, and become the firstfruits of them that slept. 1 Corinthians 15:12-13, 20

Some Corinthian believers had been preaching that there would be no resurrection from the dead. They were saying that the resurrection was not the true Biblical hope (interestingly as many "Christians" say today, saying that heaven is the hope rather than the resurrection). Paul's argument to them is "If you contend that there is no resurrection of the dead, and if you are saying that our hope is not a true bodily revival, then you are also saying that Christ has not been risen. He began the resurrection from the dead, he was the beginning and we will continue it. He was the firstfruits." Jesus' resurrection and our resurrection are the same event. They are intimately linked. He is the firstfruits. He demonstrated to us what will take place for us! He was the FIRSTBORN from the dead! What an inspiring and amazing thing it is that God, in His love, has sent His son to go before us, so that we might see in an actual person, in a MAN, the EXACT form of exaltation and glorification that we will receive. We can see a picture of our hope, we can look in the Word, read of the different things that happened to Jesus and say "that can be me." We are called to manifest the LORD now, and someday, just as Jesus does, we will do it spotlessly and flawlessly. What a gift it is to be able to know the Truth of God and to understand what He has written down. May thanks always be given to God for something so wonderful as this.

Jesus was raised from the dead, and we can be too. As we follow this next step, we see that not only can we be raised, but that God's name can be given to us, just as it was to him! THE NAME OF GOD! The name of the One who created all that we see around us. The One who controls the waves, who gives breath to all living things. We can be given His name. We can be made perfect representatives of Him. We can manifest Him and be given His authority.

GIVEN GOD'S NAME AS OUR OWN

The Biblical hope is a resurrection from the dead and living with Christ on earth (Matthew 5:5), showing the glory and character of God. In this, we will fulfill God's purpose of filling the earth with His glory. We will bring Him honor. This all comes about through the process of exaltation that we have been exploring. Jesus was our forerunner in this process, in which the final step is being called by God's name. The apostle John wrote to us about this in the book of Revelation.

> Him that overcometh will I make a pillar in the temple of my God, and he shall go no more out: and <u>I will write upon him the name of my God</u>, and the name of the city of my God, which is new Jerusalem, which cometh down out of heaven from my God: and <u>I will write upon him my new name</u>. Revelation 3:12

Those who overcome through faith will have God's name written on them. God's name will become part of who they are! When something is written on you, it becomes part of you. God's name will be on them, it will be who they are. This does not literally mean that they will have God's name tattooed on them, but instead that they will be given that name with all of its meaning, and all of its character. Just as Jesus was changed when God's name was made his, so will we be changed. The name becoming part of us is again stated in Revelation 22.

"And there shall be no more curse: but the throne of God and of the Lamb shall be in it; and his servants shall serve him: and they shall see his face; and <u>his name shall be in their foreheads</u>." Revelation 22:3-4

God will change the name of His servants so that their name is His name. This chapter tells us that "his name shall be in their foreheads." Again, this shows us that having the LORD's name written on us is symbolic. All throughout the Bible, the forehead is representative of who you are. In

Exodus 28, the Jewish high priest had to wear a gold plate on his forehead which read "Holiness to Yahweh" because that was who he was. He was the high priest, a holy and set apart vessel for God. In Revelation 17, the wicked harlot has "Mystery, Babylon the Great, the Mother of Harlots and abominations of the earth" written on her forehead. That is who she is, she is "the Mother of Harlots and abominations of the earth." When the servants of God have His name written on their foreheads, that will be who they are! They will be like Him, they will be given His authority, their characters will be changed, they will be immortal. This could be you.

WE SHALL BE LIKE HIM

When all of this takes place, when we are given the LORD's name, then we will have followed Jesus. The process will be complete. We will have gone down the same path as our Lord. We were baptized into the name, resurrected from the dead, and now actually given the name of God. We will serve our Lord, doing His bidding. Our every thought will be for the glory of God. Our characters will fit that name, and "we shall be like him."

"Beloved, now are we the sons of God, and it doth not yet appear what we shall be: but we know that, when he shall appear, we shall be like him; for we shall see him as he is." 1 John 3:2

We will see him as he is, and that will change us entirely. The apostle Peter puts it this way:

According as his divine power hath given unto us all things that pertain unto life and godliness, through the knowledge of him that hath called us to glory and

> virtue: whereby are given unto us exceeding great and precious promises: that by these <u>ye might be partakers of the divine nature</u>, having escaped the corruption that is in the world through lust. 2 Peter 1:3-4

Our bodies will be changed. Our nature will be changed. Our thoughts will be changed. We will be in the image of the Lord Jesus. We will have followed the process that he pioneered. And we shall be saved. This is repeated throughout the Bible.

"For whom he did foreknow, he also did predestinate <u>to be conformed to the image of his Son</u>, that he might be the firstborn among many brethren." Romans 8:29

We will be made in the image of Jesus. We will have followed him in the same path to glory.

> For our conversation is in heaven; from whence also we look for the Saviour, the Lord Jesus Christ: <u>who shall change our vile body, that is may be fashioned like unto his glorious body</u>, according to the working whereby he is able even to subdue all things unto himself. Philippians 3:20-21

No longer will our bodies be corruptible, filled with the lust of the flesh. We will be changed. The true believers of God will be like Jesus. And so the process will be complete. We will be glorified, lifted up, made so much better than we are at this moment. We will be given a glorious body. Don't ever let yourself forget this hope! This is what we must have before our eyes at all times, so that we can give ourselves the encouragement to fight sin, to fight spiritual wickedness in high places (Ephesians 6:12). The glory that will be given to us will make any trials or hardships that we have had to go through look pitiful, because of its greatness. We have a powerful, living hope, and its wonder will dwarf any of frustrations that we have had to go through.

"For our light affliction, which is but for a moment, <u>worketh for us a far more exceeding and eternal weight of glory.</u>" 2 Corinthians 4:17

If you feel tired by the difficulties that you are going through, if you feel shattered and don't think that you can continue trying to serve, if you feel so suppressed and beaten by sin, take heart. The best is yet to come.

TRUE LOVE

God has abundantly blessed us by inviting us to bear His name, and offering to eventually write it upon us, to have it become our name. This is a great cause of joy! There is no way that we could ever deserve something as wonderful as this! The Almighty Ruler of this universe, who holds this world, who holds my life, who holds everything I have in His hands, has asked me, and He has asked YOU to be called by His name and have a future with Him. This whole concept, this whole idea of bearing the name of God and representing Him is greatly and wonderfully complimented by the Marriage of the Lamb.

In the book of Revelation, the apostle John spoke to us of many things that were to take place. Some of those things have happened already, and some of them will happen once Christ comes back to this earth. One of the things he wrote of was the "Marriage of the Lamb," or the marriage of Jesus to his bride. This will take place soon after the return of Jesus to this earth.

"And I heard as it were the voice of a great multitude, and as the voice of many waters, and as the voice of mighty thunderings, saying, Alleluia: for the Lord God omnipotent reigneth. Let us be glad and rejoice, and give honour to him: <u>for the marriage of the Lamb is come</u>, and his wife hath made herself ready. And to her was granted that she should be arrayed in fine linen, clean and white: for the fine linen is the righteousness of saints." Revelation 19:6-8

This Marriage of the Lamb is another name for the marriage of Jesus and the believers. Jesus is the lamb and the believers are his bride. "For the fine linen is the righteousness of saints." The saints, the true believers, will be clothed with the righteousness which they have been given by God. This marriage is explained by the apostle Paul in Ephesians. He speaks of Jesus being the husband and the believers being the bride.

"For this cause shall a man leave his father and mother, and shall be joined unto his wife, and they two shall be one flesh. This is a great mystery: <u>but I speak concerning Christ and the church.</u>" Ephesians 5:31-32

Paul quotes from Genesis 2, where we are told that a man should leave his father and mother and cleave to his wife. And then, he tells us something that we may not have been expecting. "This is great mystery: but I speak concerning Christ and the church." He applies this quote to Jesus and the believers, saying that they will be married just as a husband and wife! Notice as well that he calls this oneness between a man and a woman a "great mystery," because the world doesn't understand true marriage, but the believers do! They understand what it means to be one flesh!

Connecting the steps of salvation that we discussed earlier, with this idea of a marriage, shows us that in effect, the invitation to bear the Father's name is the Lord Jesus going down on his knee and asking us to take on his name. Jesus Christ is proposing to us. It is this Jesus, the same one who said "All power is given unto me in heaven and in earth." This same Jesus is asking us, people buried in our own sin, to marry him. He is asking us to be called by his name now, and one day, eventually, take that name on as our own. We can accept this proposal, we can cry out "yes!" to Jesus by crucifying our old selves through true baptism. We can engage ourselves to Jesus, committing ourselves to him forever!

ENGAGEMENT TO CHRIST

As we are waiting for Jesus to return, we are his betrothed. We are waiting for our husband to come and take us as his own. And at the same time, by baptism and by bearing the name, we are telling our Father, and we are telling Christ that we will strive to live in the way that they desire. We will strive to take on their characteristics! As someone engaged to the greatest husband we can know, we are pledging that we will strive to be a pure bride for when he comes. We will strive to be one mind, one spirit, and one heart with Christ.

Just as it is when we are called by God's name, so it is when we are engaged. We are associated with God, we are associated with Christ. Thus, the things that we do can affect the way that people see our betrothed. In addition to this, not only are our actions important, our beliefs are as well. Our beliefs and actions determine whether or not we will be a pure virgin for Jesus. Paul spoke of this when he wrote to the Corinthians:

> "For I am jealous over you with godly jealousy: for I have espoused you to one husband, that I may present you as a chaste virgin to Christ. But I fear, lest by any means, as the serpent beguiled Eve through his subtilty, so your minds should be corrupted from the simplicity that is in Christ. For if he that cometh preacheth another Jesus, whom we have not preached, or if ye receive another spirit, which ye have not received, or another gospel, which ye have not accepted, ye might well bear with him.
> 2 Corinthians 11:2-4

Paul really wanted the Corinthians to understand that what they believed and did was so important! He began by saying that he had jealousy over the believers that he had converted in Corinth. He had brought them to Jesus by teaching them the gospel, and led them to engagement, waiting to be married to Christ. Now, he felt a "godly jealousy" or zeal for their salvation. So Paul says, "You are engaged to Christ, and I want to present you to him when he comes. He is going to come to take you as his wife, and I want to be able to give you to him as someone that has kept themselves clean from other men, as a chaste virgin." But in verse 3, he was afraid that he might not be able to do so. Just as the serpent tricked Eve in the garden, it seemed as though the believers were being led astray from the simple truth that can be found in Jesus, or "the simplicity that is in Christ." They were starting to hear and believe other doctrines that are not true at all. Verse 4 says, "For if he that cometh preacheth another Jesus, whom we have not preached, or if ye receive another spirit, which we have not received, or another gospel, which ye have not accepted, ye might well bear with him." They were allowing these people to come into their body and preach things that were totally untrue, preach things about Jesus that were flat out wrong, things that angered God to hear, falsities about Him, things that slandered who He really was. They were preaching a different Jesus, and a different gospel. If the saints at Corinth believed these things, they would defile themselves and not be pure for Jesus! But, if they stayed in the Truth, then they would be that pure virgin, ready to be with Christ and be united with him in marriage when he came. But, if they put their beliefs in false doctrines, in things that were not true, then they would be a defiled bride. This was a serious accusation.

The apostles wanted the people to see that if they started believing another gospel, or did not believe the truth about Jesus (falsehoods, such as the Trinity) then they would be a defiled bride! They would not be pure! Imagine what that would be like. Say that you did not follow the Truth of God's word, and so you lost your purity, you lost your innocence as a bride for Jesus. That would be the worst feeling that you could possibly feel. That would be the worst day of your life. Imagine seeing Jesus, who has waited to be your husband, who died so that you could live, who is so excited to be united with you, and looking into his eyes when he knows that you weren't pure, when he knows that you defiled yourself with churches preaching falsehoods and lies! Stay pure, cleave to Scripture!

This is an important point that we must emphasize. God cares very much about our beliefs. If we know the Truth and yet choose to believe something different, God sees this as us defiling ourselves and sleeping around. He sees this as us rejecting His son, losing our purity, and selling ourselves to others. This is something of vast importance. This is something to which we must take heed. If we understand this, then we cannot promote false doctrines or those who teach them. We cannot associate ourselves with them. We cannot be baptized into churches that teach these things. They are defiling, their teachings are false gods that we will be "sleeping with" if we support them. This is why the apostle John takes such a firm stance about the system that he calls "antichrist" in 2nd John. Originally, he was speaking of the Gnostics, people who taught lies about Jesus and about God, but the things that he says about the antichrist system have a dual application to the religions of today, which hold to the teaching of the Trinity (notice that the Antichrist is not a future ruler, it was present at the time of John—2 John 1:7. In addition, it would teach that Jesus did not come in the flesh— 1 John 4:3; the Trinity teaches this when it states that Jesus was God Himself and did not have the urge to ever sin. The flesh comes with temptation, and to deny the temptations of Jesus, as the Trinity does, is to say that Jesus did not come in the flesh). He says to not even let people who teach things like this into your house! He says not to wish them God speed because that makes you a partaker of their EVIL DEEDS (2 John 1:7-11)! This was something that was so dear to the apostle's heart. He did not want his brothers and sisters to be a defiled bride for their husband. They had to understand the implications and the impact that false teaching could have on them. They had to stay together as people who knew the Truth, who could encourage one another in it, and who could strengthen each other to preach the gospel. If the things that you have read in this book have convicted you of the truth of God manifestation, and have been sufficiently proven by Scripture, then I implore you to not turn back to the false

"Christian" systems that teach blasphemies, such as the Trinity. Hold to your true understanding of the gospel, never let it go, and find a group of believers who cleave to the enlightening teaching of the Word of God. Find a group of believers who understand the true relationship between the Father and the Son, and study for baptism. Search out the nearest group of Christadelphians, and keep pouring through the Scriptures. May you esteem the things of the world, its popularity, its glory, its riches, as loss for the sake of knowing Christ.

Because, you don't have to stand before our Lord as an impure "virgin." You don't have to look through mournful, tear-stained eyes when you stand before him. You don't have to believe the false things that Christendom teaches today. Those who are engaged and who stay pure, will be united in a glorious, joyful, and beautiful marriage when he returns. They will be made one with Jesus, and "the two shall be one flesh"!

ONE WITH THE LORD JESUS

We can be united with him. We can be one with the Messiah sent from heaven, with the son of God. We can share his same goals and character. Christ can help us align our hearts and our purpose with his and our vile bodies can be changed to be like his. We can be in his image. We shall be like him. Let us just read Ephesians 5 once again to remind of us this great day:

"For this cause shall a man leave his father and mother, and shall be joined unto his wife, and they two shall be one flesh. This is a great mystery: but I speak concerning Christ and the church." Ephesians 5:31-32

There will be a day when Jesus holds fast to his wife. What a beautiful thought! I have such a hard time even comprehending what it will be like to be one with Jesus! Things within me, within you, will have to change so much! There are so many parts of me that are not in line with God, that need to be fixed. But they will be changed. And what an exciting and joyous thought this is. Not only is it exciting for us, but Jesus is excited about this time as well. Psalm 45 is a psalm that applies to this marriage between us and Christ.

"<u>So shall the king greatly desire thy beauty</u>: for he is thy Lord; and worship thou him." Psalm 45:11

The king, the Lord Jesus, will greatly desire our beauty! He will look upon us with joy and excitement! We read of this same thing in Song of Solomon. This is a book written by King Solomon to one of his brides and it is also a beautiful description of our marriage to Jesus. In it, the groom, Jesus Christ, says to us,

> You have captivated my heart, my sister, my bride; you have captivated my heart with one glance of your eyes, with one jewel of your necklace. How beautiful is your love, my sister, my bride! How much better is your love than wine, and the fragrance of your oils than any spice! Song of Solomon 4:9-10 *English Standard Version*

I can just image him saying this to us. Once our thoughts and our characters have been changed; once sin has been completely trampled by God, I can image Jesus looking into our eyes, smiling, holding our hands, saying to us "you have captivated my heart…" The Lord Jesus is in love with us. Our sins will be wiped away, and even the desire to sin will be destroyed. Never again will we be tempted to lie, never again will we be tempted to act selfishly. Our nastiness, our filthiness from our sins, they will all be gone! Our sinful nature will be wiped away and replaced with the nature of our Father.

"The king's daughter is all glorious within: her clothing is of wrought gold." Psalm 45:13

She is "all glorious within." Her character is beautiful. Our character will be beautiful. And, just as at a marriage today, when we are united with him, when our sins are wiped away, our names will be changed. Your name won't mean the same thing anymore. You will be given the name of God, the name of Christ your husband. And just as we read in Revelation 3:12, "I will write upon him...my new name." That name will become a part of us. It will be written upon us.

CONCLUDING THOUGHTS

The name of God, Yahweh, will be written upon us as it is on Jesus, if we continue in the faith. He revealed God's character to us, and by the Father's grace, we will one day be able to reveal that character perfectly to others. We are walking that same path that Jesus took to glory, and eventually we will meet him. Those of us who are baptized into the Truth have accepted the invitation to do this. We have accepted Jesus' proposal. We have said "yes!" to our king. Someday, if we stay in the way of Truth, we will be a pure virgin for our love, and we shall be like him. We will be wondrously and gloriously united with him! We will be joined together with one heart and one goal! God's character will be displayed through all of us. He will be manifested, and people will praise Him because they will see His goodness through us. His honor and His glory will fill the whole earth. We look for that day, with excitement and anticipation, waiting to be made one with our beloved!

UNITED WITH CHRIST

A Summary

1. What is the difference between being called by a name and actually possessing that name?

2. Jesus has been given God's name. Give one verse to prove this:
   _____

3. We cannot follow Jesus down his path of glory. True/False

4. How can we be called by God's name?

5. Fill in the blank: Just as Jesus was _____ by God's name, we can be as well. Just as Jesus was _____ and given immortality, we can also be. Finally, Jesus _____ the name of God. Revelation 3:12 tells us that we can also do this.

6. List three verses that speak of us being made like Jesus:
   _____   _____
   _____

7. Fill in the blank: In Ephesians _____, Paul tells us that we can be married to Jesus.

8. Multiple Choice:
   How can we stay a beautiful bride for Christ?
   a. By neglecting the Bible and doing what we want
   b. By believing the Truth of the gospel and holding to it
   c. By believing the Trinity
   d. It's a mystery
   e. Getting our hair done up nicely

ANSWERS:

1. When you are called by a name, it doesn't have to be who you truly are. You just did something to be associated with the name. When you possess a name, it is who you really are.
2. Philippians 2:8-11
3. False
4. True Baptism
5. Called; raised; possesses
6. Any of the verses from pg. 109-110
7. 5:32
8. b.

CHAPTER 6

"AND THE WORD WAS MADE FLESH"

As students of the Word, as those who are trying to spread the Truth to all civilization, it is important for us to know passages that are used by Trinitarians and to know how to explain them in the light of the Truth. John 1:1-14 is one such passage. These verses are very often used to prove the Trinity and Christ's preexistence. This chapter is going to focus on explaining the apostle's writing in a consistent and logical manner. Contrary to what many may say, John 1 is not at all teaching the preexistence of Christ. It is not saying that Jesus is the same substance as his Father. Instead, as we examine these verses, we will see that they teach us something very different. When we can understand the truth of this passage, it will help us to be more confident when trying to explain it to those around us.

Here is the text of John 1:1-14 so that you may become familiar with it.

> In the beginning was the Word, and the Word was with God, and the Word was God. The same was in the beginning with God. All things were made by him; and without him was not any thing made that was made. In him was life; and the life was the light of

men. And the light shineth in darkness; and the darkness comprehended it not. There was a man sent from God, whose name was John. The same came for a witness, to bear witness of the Light, that all men through him might believe. He was not that Light, but was sent to bear witness of that Light. That was the true Light, which lighteth every man that cometh into the world. He was in the world, and the world was made by him, and the world knew him not. He came unto his own, and his own received him not. But as many as received him, to them gave he power to become the sons of God, even to them that believe on his name: which were born, not of blood, nor of the will of the flesh, nor of the will of man, but of God. And the Word was made flesh, and dwelt among us, (and we beheld his glory, the glory as of the only begotten of the Father,) full of grace and truth. John 1:1-14

In my experience, a Trinitarian would explain the passage in this way: "We can see that Jesus is the Word, as said in verse 14. We are told in verses 1-3 that the Word was God, that it was with God in the beginning, and that the Word created all things. If Jesus was the Word, then we are being told that Jesus was with God in the beginning and that he is responsible for creation. In addition to this, this case is backed up by the fact that 'the Word' is called 'him' throughout the first few verses, which makes it sound as though it is a person, namely Jesus." No doubt that this is a fairly difficult passage for us to fit in with the rest of Scripture. The Bible clearly teaches that Jesus is subordinate to God, clearly teaches that he was a representative of God. To add to this, Jesus is not present in the Old Testament except in prophecy. Therefore, what does John 1 really mean?

In order to answer this question, we will be looking at a few different connections. Mainly we will study the themes of John's gospel, take an in-depth look at the word "Word," and discuss Greek pronouns. At the end of this chapter, you should have a logical and Scriptural method in which to explain John 1.

The Purpose of John's Gospel

John 1:1-14 is the beginning of the gospel; it is the introduction to the book. A key to understanding the introductions of many of the books of the Bible is to understand the theme of that book. Quite often, the beginning of a book will quickly summarize the information that follows or will set forth a topic that will be covered in the pages that proceed. The same is true of the gospel of John. Its introduction lays out the theme of the entire book; when we can understand the theme of the 20 other chapters in John, then this knowledge will greatly help us to understand the meaning of the first few verses of the first chapter.

The gospel of John is unlike any other gospel. In it, we find an intimate look at the thoughts of our Lord, being able to hear many of his last words to his disciples before his death. It is a book of emotion, and a book that is very figurative. Reading through the gospel, certain themes stand out. John's gospel seems to have at least two themes:

1. *Jesus spoke God's words*
2. *Jesus is the son of God*

A SPEAKER OF GOD'S WORDS

John had a very strong emphasis on Jesus speaking God's words. He repeatedly showed us incidents of Jesus saying that his words were not his own, but his Father's. You may have noticed in chapter 4 of this book, how often John was quoted, especially when we were referring to Jesus speaking his Father's teaching. It came up time and time again. Here are some of the references once again:

"<u>For he whom God hath sent speaketh the words of God</u>: for God giveth not the Spirit by measure unto him." John 3:34

"Jesus answered them, and said, <u>My doctrine is not mine, but his that sent me</u>. If any man will do his will, he shall know of the doctrine, whether it be of God, or whether I speak of myself." John 7:16-17

"Believest thou not that I am in the Father, and the Father in me? <u>The words that I speak unto you I speak not of myself: but the Father that dwelleth in me</u>, he doeth the works." John 14:10

"<u>For I have given unto them the words which thou gavest me</u>; and they have received them, and have known surely that I came out from thee, and they have believed that thou didst send me." John 17:8

This idea, that Jesus is not speaking his own words, but his Father's, is very frequently seen in John. Other references that say this same thing are: John 8:26, 28, 38, 46-47; John 12:49-50; John 14:24; John 15:15; John 17:14. The apostle was trying to show his readers that a very special person had come. Unlike any other, this man would constantly speak divine words. John was trying to show them that this person that had come was a beaming and glorious representative of the God of Israel. He was a mediator to the people and to the world, speaking to them the words of his Father. Closely connected with this purpose, another purpose of the apostle's gospel was showing that Jesus is the son of God.

JESUS IS THE SON OF GOD

John makes no small effort to show his readers that Jesus is the son of God. His book is the gospel that has the most open proclamations of Jesus' sonship, both by Christ himself and also by others. On top of this fact, John has almost as many indirect references to Jesus being God's son and God being his Father as all three of the other gospels put together. Let us go through the comparisons together.

Throughout the gospel of John, people are testifying that Jesus is God's son. This begins early on in the book, first occurring in the section that we are examining:

"And The Word was made flesh, and dwelt among us, (and we beheld his glory, <u>the glory as of the only begotten of the Father,</u>) full of grace and truth." John 1:14

In fact, chapter 1 has three occasions in which various people are proclaiming Jesus as the son of God. The next person to do this is John the Baptist.

"And I saw, and bare record that this is <u>the Son of God</u>." John 1:34

A few verses later, as Jesus begins to call his disciples, Nathaniel meets him. Nathaniel's question to Christ is "How do you know me?" Jesus responds to him by saying "I saw you while you were under the fig tree before Philip called you." Somehow, there was something remarkable about this answer and Nathaniel realized the one before whom he was standing:

"Nathanael answered and saith unto him, Rabbi, thou art the Son of God; thou art the King of Israel." John 1:49

The next proclamation is the end of John 6. Jesus had fed the multitude and the next day told them to seek for the true bread, himself. He told them to eat of his body and to drink his blood, which offended many of them. Very many of his disciples left from that moment on. Upon their departure, Jesus looked at Peter and speaking of the 12 disciples, said, "Will you leave also?" Peter's answer contained this testimony:

"And we believe and are sure that thou art that Christ, the Son of the living God." John 6:69

Later, Jesus was in the area where John had first begun baptizing. At the same time, Lazarus, the brother of Martha and Mary, became extremely sick and the two sisters sent to Christ, trying to get him to come over and heal their brother. Jesus, because of his love for them, stayed for a few days in the place where he was, so that he come later and raise up Lazarus. When he finally arrived at their house, Martha ran out to meet him and within their dialogue, she declared her belief that he was the son of God.

"She saith unto him, Yea, Lord: I believe that thou art the Christ, the Son of God, which should come into the world." John 11:27

The gospel of John contains FIVE instances in which people

proclaimed Jesus to be God's son. This is extremely different than the references from the other gospels. In all of the synoptic gospels put together, you read of only SIX incidents in which sane people acknowledged that he was the son of God (including double incidents, such as the centurion in Matthew and Mark):

1. *After calming the storm (Matthew 14:33)*
2. *Peter testifying who Jesus is (Matthew 16:16)*
3. *The centurion at the cross (Matthew 27:54)*
4. *The introduction of Mark's gospel (Mark 1:1)*
5. *The centurion at the cross (Mark 15:39)*
6. *Gabriel when speaking to Mary (Luke 1:35)*

Thus, excluding times in which the demon-possessed referred to Jesus as the son of God (since their testimony probably would not have carried much weight with the readers), John's gospel has almost as many references to people calling Jesus the son of God as the rest of the gospels put together! This must have been a focus of John's writing. We will notice this same type of trend when we look at all of the times in which Jesus called himself the son of God in the synoptic gospels compared to the gospel of John.

The first occurrence of this is actually when Jesus is speaking with the Jews, just after the time when he healed the man who had been lame for 38 years. Jesus said:

"Verily, verily, I say unto you, The hour is coming, and now is, when the dead shall hear the voice of the Son of God: and they that hear shall live." John 5:25

In another discussion with the Jews, Jesus reinforces this point that he was God's son. He states that he came forth from

God. This is another way of saying that God was his Father.

"Jesus said unto them, If God were your Father, ye would love me: for <u>I proceeded forth and came from God</u>; neither came I of myself, but he sent me." John 8:42

Later, after being chased out of the temple by the Jews, he healed a man who had been blind from his birth. This happened on the Sabbath. The man was taken in front of the Jews, having to testify about his healing and what he thought of the healer. He made a valiant defense for his faith, being expelled from the synagogue because of his belief in Christ. Just after this, Jesus met him and told him of his sonship.

> Jesus heard that they had cast him out; and when he had found him, he said unto him, Dost thou believe on <u>the Son of God</u>? He answered and said, Who is he, Lord, that I might believe on him? And Jesus said unto him, Thou hast both seen him, and <u>it is he that talketh with thee</u>. And he said, Lord, I believe. And he worshipped him. John 9:35-38

Another time, as we saw in the chapter about Jesus and God manifestation, he was talking to the Jews about his Father and being one with Him. This was misunderstood by them. They took it just as many Trinitarians take it today, that he was saying that he was God. In reality, as Jesus explained to them, he was only saying that they were one mind (since he was God's son) and if he had called himself God (as they accused), there really would not have been a problem anyway because of God manifestation.

"Say ye of him, whom the Father hath sanctified, and sent into the world, Thou blasphemest; because I said, <u>I am the</u>

Son of God?" John 10:36

We have already looked at the death and resurrection of Lazarus. Jesus calls himself the "Son of God" in the beginning of that story, right when he found out about Lazarus' sickness. The following was his response:

"When Jesus heard that, he said, This sickness is not unto death, but for the glory of God, that <u>the Son of God</u> might be glorified thereby." John 11:4

The last time in which Jesus referred to himself as the son of God in John's gospel was just before his crucifixion. He was speaking some of his last words to his disciples, and he reminds them that he came forth from the Father.

"For the Father himself loveth you, because ye have loved me, and have believed that I came out from God. <u>I came forth from the Father</u>, and am come into the world: again, I leave the world, and go to the Father." John 16:27-28

All together, there are six times in which Jesus testifies that he is the son of God in the gospel of John. Here is where these statistics become powerful. Compare these results to the rest of the gospels put together. Even when combining all three of the other gospels, there are only three times in which Jesus says that he is the son of God and they are all in the same incident, his trial before his death.

1. *When questioned by the Jewish council before his crucifixion (Matthew 26:63)*
2. *When questioned by the Jewish council before his crucifixion (Mark 14:61-62)*

3. *When questioned by the Jewish council before his crucifixion (Luke 22:70)*

Six times Jesus calls himself the son of God in John's gospel! He only does this three times in the other gospels put together! And the other gospels are all speaking of the SAME incident! In addition to this, each gospel has indirect references to Jesus being God's son, such as the writer calling Jesus "the son" or Christ calling God "my Father." When counting up all of these in each gospel, the trend stays true. Take some time to look at the following tables:

Indirect References in Matthew to Jesus being God's son:

1. Matthew 2:15	2. Matthew 3:17
3. Matthew 14:33	4. Matthew 17:5
5. Matthew 21:37	6. Matthew 22:2
7. Matthew 22:42	8. Matthew 28:19
9. Matthew 8:29	10. Matthew 11:27
11. Matthew 11:27	12. Matthew 11:27
13. Matthew 16:16	14. Matthew 21:37
15. Matthew 21:38	16. Matthew 22:45
17. Matthew 26:63-64	18. Matthew 27:43
19. Matthew 27:54	

Indirect References in Matthew's Gospel to God being Jesus' Father:

1. Matthew 7:21	2. Matthew 10:32
3. Matthew 12:50	4. Matthew 15:13
5. Matthew 16:27	6. Matthew 18:10
7. Matthew 18:19	8. Matthew 18:35
9. Matthew 20:23	10. Matthew 24:36
11. Matthew 25:34	12. Matthew 26:29
13. Matthew 26:39	14. Matthew 26:53
15. Matthew 10:33	16. Matthew 11:25
17. Matthew 11:26	18. Matthew 11:27
19. Matthew 16:17	20. Matthew 26:42

Total: 39

Indirect References in Mark to Jesus being God's son:

1. Mark 1:11	2. Mark 9:7
3. Mark 12:6	4. Mark 12:37
5. Mark 13:32	6. Mark 1:1
7. Mark 3:11	8. Mark 5:7
9. Mark 12:6	10. Mark 14:61-62
11. Mark 15:39	

Indirect References in Mark's Gospel to God being Jesus' Father:

1. Mark 8:38	2. Mark 14:36

Total: 13

Indirect References in Luke to Jesus being God's son:

1. Luke 3:22	2. Luke 9:35
3. Luke 10:22	4. Luke 20:13
5. Luke 20:41	6. Luke 1:32
7. Luke 1:35	8. Luke 4:41
9. Luke 8:28	10. Luke 10:22
11. Luke 10:22	12. Luke 20:44
13. Luke 22:70	

References in Luke's Gospel to God being Jesus' Father:

1. Luke 10:21	2. Luke 2:49
3. Luke 9:26	4. Luke 10:21
5. Luke 22:29	6. Luke 22:42
7. Luke 23:34	8. Luke 23:46
9. Luke 24:49	10. Luke 10:22

Total: 23

"AND THE WORD WAS MADE FLESH"

Indirect References in John to Jesus being God's son:

1. John 1:18	2. John 3:16
3. John 3:35	4. John 5:19
5. John 6:40	6. John 8:36
7. John 14:13	8. John 17:1
9. John 1:34	10. John 1:49
11. John 3:17	12. John 3:18
12. John 3:36	14. John 3:36
15. John 5:19	16. John 5:20
17. John 5:21	18. John 5:22
19. John 5:23	20. John 5:25
21. John 5:26	22. John 6:69
23. John 9:35-38	24. John 10:36
25. John 11:4	26. John 11:27
27. John 17:1	28. John 20:31

Indirect References in John's Gospel to God being Jesus' Father:

1. John 2:16	2. John 6:32
3. John 10:29	4. John 20:7
5. John 5:17	6. John 6:65
7. John 5:18	8. John 5:43

9. John 8:19	10. John 8:28
11. John 20:17	12. John 8:38
13. John 8:49	14. John 8:54
15. John 18:11	16. John 10:17
17. John 10:18	18. John 10:25
19. John 10:29	20. John 17:25
21. John 10:32	22. John 10:37
23. John 11:41	24. John 17:24
25. John 12:27	26. John 12:28
27. John 14:2	28. John 14:7
29. John 14:12	30. John 14:20
31. John 14:21	32. John 14:23
33. John 14:28	34. John 15:1
35. John 15:8	36. John 15:10
37. John 15:15	38. John 15:23
39. John 15:24	40. John 16:10
41. John 17:1	42. John 17:5
43. John 17:11	44. John 17:21

Total: 72

Matthew + Mark + Luke = 75
John = 72

Again, when all of the synoptic gospels are combined, it can easily been seen that John has almost as many references to Jesus' sonship as all of the others put together! John has more testimonies which state that Jesus is the son of God than any of the other gospels. He has more indirect references to Jesus being God's son and God being Jesus' Father than any other gospel. Clearly, from the study we have done, the apostle's theme is that Jesus is the son of God, along with Jesus being a man who spoke God's words. In whatever way we understand John's introduction, it needs to fit within these two purposes of his gospel.

WHAT IS THE WORD?

We now know the themes of John's gospel: Jesus spoke God's words, and he is God's son. When we develop a way of explaining John 1, it needs to fit in with both of those purposes. Keeping this in mind, let us begin to examine the first few verses of John 1.

> In the beginning was the Word, and the Word was with God, and the Word was God. The same was in the beginning with God. All things were made by him; and without him was not any thing made that was made. In him was life; and the life was the light of men. And the light shineth in darkness; and the darkness comprehended it not. John 1:1-5

Look through these initial statements that begin the fourth gospel. One of the first questions that comes to mind is, "If Scripture is speaking here of Jesus, why does it call him the Word? In fact, why does it use 'the Word' here as the main character? What is 'the Word'? Why doesn't it just say 'Jesus'?" Understanding this question is essential to a proper understanding of what this passage is telling us. "The Word" is the main focus of attention here in these first few sentences, and if we don't know what Word this is, then we will miss the whole point of the section.

A quick word study on "the Word" can be extremely enlightening. In the Greek, it is the word "logos." Sometimes "logos" is translated as different words in English based off of what it means in the Greek. Therefore, by looking at the different ways it has been translated into English, we can get a broader idea of what "logos" could possibly mean in addition to "word." Going through the different places that it is used, the context seems to indicate that it means "teaching" or "doctrine" or "sayings":

"And he said unto them, What things? And they said unto him, Concerning Jesus of Nazareth, which was a prophet mighty in deed and <u>word</u> before God and all the people." Luke 24:19

"When therefore he was risen from the dead, his disciples remembered that he had said this unto them; and they believed the scripture, and <u>the word</u> which Jesus had said." John 2:22

"And ye have not his <u>word</u> abiding in you: for whom he hath sent, him ye believe not." John 5:38

"Why do ye not understand my speech? even because ye cannot hear my <u>word</u>." John 8:43

"For this cause also thank we God without ceasing, because, when ye received <u>the word</u> of God which ye heard of us, ye received it not as <u>the word</u> of men, but as it is in truth, <u>the word</u> of God, which effectually worketh also in you that believe." 1 Thessalonians 2:13

In addition to meaning "sayings" or "teachings" it can also mean "purpose." The underlined word "intent" is the same Greek word "logos."

"Therefore came I unto you without gainsaying, as soon as I was sent for: I ask therefore for what <u>intent</u> ye have sent for me?" Acts 10:29

"Logos" can mean a few different things. Mainly, it can mean teachings and sayings, or purpose and intent. We see words with multiple definitions in English as well. We can have one word that means many different things, some of the meanings may be connected, and some may be completely separate. For example, think of the word "book." Very easily, and very correctly, we could tell our friend or spouse "I am going to read my favorite book this week." But, "book" can also mean something very different, such as "I will book my airline tickets this afternoon." Just recently, I was speaking to a friend about the Holy Spirit and all of its different roles. He looked at me and said, "well, what does the word 'light' mean?" My answer was, "I would say illumination." "No, when I said 'light,' I was referring to something that didn't weigh very much," was his reply. "This is how the word 'spirit' is used in the Bible, sometimes it means 'mind' other times it is referring to 'power.' Just as 'light' can mean illumination and also lightweight, 'spirit' can mean different things as well." We see the same thing when we look at "logos." Sometimes it can refer to teachings, sometimes it can refer to purpose. In addition, since we do not speak Greek, it could also have another meaning that we have not yet seen. From our word study, "logos" in this passage may mean:

1. *Sayings or teaching*
2. *Purpose or intent*
3. Another meaning which we have not yet seen

Thus, we must take our definitions of this word 'logos' and compare them to the context of John 1 to see how they fit what has been said. We cannot just plug in our definitions arbitrarily, because our definition might not fit the context at all. However, before studying 'logos' as meaning #3, we will first see if any of the definitions that we do have, fit. Here are our verses once again:

> In the beginning was the Word, and the Word was with God, and the Word was God. The same was in the beginning with God. All things were made by him; and without him was not any thing made that was made. In him was life; and the life was the light of men. And the light shineth in darkness; and the darkness comprehended it not. John 1:1-5

In these verses we read about a Word. In the beginning the Word was with God. This seems to work so far with all of the definitions that we have. God's saying and teaching have been with Him from the beginning (Genesis 1:3). Also, His purpose has been with Him from the beginning (see Matthew 25:34). This Word was also called "God." It was Him. Again, with the idea of God's sayings, definition #1, it fits. His sayings and teachings were part of Him. They are basically His mind spoken out to His angels and to mortal man. His doctrine is who He is; His teaching is part of Himself. The same logic works for His purpose, definition #2. All of His thoughts and plans are part of who He is, they are part of His mind. Both of these definitions are in accord with the first two verses.

In verse 3, we read of all things being made by this Word and it is emphasized to us that everything that was created was made by the Word. When looking at our two definitions, it seems that definition #1, the "sayings" of God fits perfectly. God's "purpose" may be said to have <u>led</u> to the creation of all things, but it does not appear that His purpose actually created all things. Definition #2 does not fit as well. Instead, the testimony of Scripture is clear to the role of God's sayings in creation.

"By the word of the LORD were the heavens made; and all the host of them by the breath of his mouth." Psalm 33:6

"Through faith we understand that the worlds were framed by the word of God, so that things which are seen were not made of things which do appear." Hebrews 11:3

"For this they willingly are ignorant of, that by the word of God the heavens were of old, and the earth standing out of the water and in the water." 2 Peter 3:5

These verses are speaking of God's spoken word, His sayings. We know this when we look back to the record of Genesis. As we read through chapter 1, one of the phrases that continuously appears is "and God said…" and then something was created. God's sayings created all things. His WORD was a vital part of the creation process. He spoke and it was done. Comparing our two definitions to verse 3, it seems fairly apparent as to the one that is being used in these verses. But, before we choose one, let us continue to compare the verses and the definitions.

Verses 4 and 5 tell us some important characteristics of this Word. They tell us that the Word was life, and in addition, it was not comprehended by the darkness. Again, this fits well with God's "purpose." His purpose has brought life, and "the darkness," or those who are ignorant, do not seem to understand it. But it fits perfectly with the idea of God's "teachings" or "sayings." God's teachings were life:

"This is my comfort in my affliction: for <u>thy word hath quickened me</u>." Psalm 119:50

"Holding forth <u>the word of life</u>; that I may rejoice in the day of Christ, that I have not run in vain, neither laboured in vain." Philippians 2:16

The teaching of God is life. Through His sayings, people can understand the things that they need for salvation. God's teaching brings life to those who believe it. From verse 5 of John 1, the Word has also not been "comprehended" by the darkness. The darkness could not understand it. This is what we see with God's sayings. The wicked of this world cannot understand what they mean.

"He that is of God heareth God's words: ye therefore hear them not, because ye are not of God." John 8:47

The Jews often could not understand what Jesus was saying, including this incident. In this verse, Christ is saying "those who are of God can understand and believe the things that I am saying. You cannot understand them because you are wicked." He obviously was not speaking of literal hearing, because the Jews could hear him very well, hence their arguing with him (also compare what Jesus says in verse 43).

In the end after looking at the two definitions and comparing them to the chapter, John 1 seems to be speaking about God's "sayings" or His actual spoken words. Instead of speaking of the Lord Jesus Christ, instead of speaking of a person, this chapter is speaking of the power of God's spoken word. It is speaking of God's word in creation, when He said "Let it be done" and it was done. It was speaking of God's teaching, which is eternal life. Try to look through the passage again with this new understanding, and see how logical it is. The Truth of the Scriptures is a wonderful thing, with its logic and powerful Scriptural backing; unlike the lie of the Trinity, which is incomprehensible and remains a "mystery" to many. In the beginning was the teaching, the teaching was with God and the teaching was God...all things were made by His sayings...

> In the beginning was the Word, and the Word was
> with God, and the Word was God. The same was in
> the beginning with God. All things were made by
> him; and without him was not any thing made that
> was made. In him was life; and the life was the light of
> men. And the light shineth in darkness; and the
> darkness comprehended it not. John 1:1-5

The "logos" of John 1 was not a person, but instead the actual, literal words that God spoke and taught. However, mainstream Christians might tend to look at this explanation of John 1 and object, because the verses that we read make the Word sound as though it were a person. "All things were made by him." You might have had the same objection to this issue. This objection can be easily resolved through more study.

UNDERSTANDING GREEK PRONOUNS

Upon looking at the Greek language, it becomes fairly easy to pinpoint why the "Word" is called a "him," and why it sounds as though it is some type of being. This is because the Greek language ascribes a gender to each of its nouns. Thus, every noun (like "word") can either be considered male, female, or neuter, regardless of whether or not it is actually alive and has a literal gender. In Greek, "logos" is a masculine word, and so any word that refers to it will be masculine in the Greek, such as any pronouns (him, he, his). Here are few selections from different writers who are proficient in Greek:

> In the Greek, the Latin, and even modern languages, what grammarians call gender is <u>artificial</u> [meaning that it is arbitrary, a noun just has a gender regardless of whether or not it is alive]… if after having predicated of or alluded to a thing, in a preceding sentence or member of one, that is masculine, feminine, or neuter, you proceed afterwards to point out or refer to it in another by a pronoun; you must adhere, in the pronoun, to the gender of the object which it is your intention to indicate.
> In the English language the distinction of artificial gender (except in the case of a ship) is unknown as to nouns; animated things only are susceptible of distinction, as masculine or feminine. *An Etymological Essay on the Grammatical Sense in the Greek of the Sacred Texts Regarding the Last Supper*; John Joseph Dillon; Pgs. 15-16

"In Greek, very many Nouns, <u>which have no reference to *Sex*</u>, are *Masculine* or *Feminine.*" *A Greek and English Lexicon to the New Testament*; John Parkhurst; Pg. 4

Combine this quotation with the following:

"A substantive pronoun agrees with its antecedent in gender, number, and person (so far as expressed in inflection); an adjective pronoun agrees with the noun it modifies in gender, number, and case." *A Greek Grammar for Schools and Colleges*; Herbert Weir Smyth; Pg 219

Greek gives all of its nouns a gender, thus any pronoun has to agree in gender with its noun even if the noun is a thing and realistically has no gender. Occasionally we do this type of thing in English. As the first reference mentioned, imagine that we are speaking about a ship, we may say something along the lines of "she really is a beauty." Regardless of the fact that the ship is not a woman, we have arbitrarily given it a feminine gender by calling it a "she." Greek does this same type of thing with ALL of its nouns. For those of us who know other languages, Spanish does this same thing.

English does not typically have genders that it ascribes to its nouns. Instead, gender is determined by the noun itself, whether it is a person (which could be a "he" or a "she") or a place or thing (which would be an "it"). Because of this difference in the languages, it is customary for the translators to change the pronouns so that the sentence makes more sense in the English. Therefore, because "word" is a THING in English, and not a PERSON, its pronoun would normally be changed to "it" (hence why "word" is normally referred to as "it" instead of "him" in Scripture). In some translations, the translators have actually done that. These passages read:

"In the beginning was the word and the word was with God: and the word was God. The same was in the beginning with God. <u>All things were made by it and with out it was made nothing that was made</u>. In it was life and the life was ye light of men and the light shineth in the darkness but the darkness comprehended it not." John 1:1-5 Tyndale

"In the beginning was the Logos, and the Logos was with God, and the Logos was God. This was in the Beginning with God. <u>Through it everything was done; and without it not even one things was done, which has been done</u>. In it was Life; and the Life was the Light of men. And the Light shone in the darkness, and the darkness apprehended it not." John 1:1-5 Diaglott

"In the beginning was the word, and the word was with God: and that word was God. The same was in the beginning with God. <u>All things were made by it: and without it, was made nothing that was made</u>. In it was life, and the life was the light of men, and the light shineth in darkness: and the darkness comprehended it not." John 1:1-5 Bishop's 1568

"In the beginning was the word, and the word was with God and that word was God. The same was in the beginning with God. <u>All things were made by it and without was made nothing that was made</u>. In it was life, and the life was the light of men. And the light shineth in darkness and the darkness comprehended it not." John 1:1-5 Geneva 1590

You will notice that the "word" is always referred to as "it" in these translations. This makes the passage easier to understand and is more true to what the passage was trying to express in the beginning. Again, this fits perfectly with what we have seen the "word" to represent. God's sayings are an "it" and not a "him." It is unfortunate that many translations have chosen to keep the pronoun "him" in John 1, because it is misleading and tends to make readers think that this passage is supporting the doctrine of the Trinity. However, when we understand that the passage should read "it" instead of "him," the verses are much more understandable.

Now that we have a better grasp of verses 1-5, let us move on. Here is the selection again, beginning at verse 6.

> There was a man sent from God, whose name was John. The same came for a witness, to bear witness of the Light, that all men through him might believe. He was not that Light, but was sent to bear witness of that Light. That was the true Light, which lighteth every man that cometh into the world. He was in the world, and the world was made by him, and the world knew him not. He came unto his own, and his own received him not. But as many as received him, to them gave he power to become the sons of God, even to them that believe on his name: which were born, not of blood, nor of the will of the flesh, nor of the will of man, but of God. And the Word was made flesh, and dwelt among us, (and we beheld his glory, the glory as of the only begotten of the Father,) full of grace and truth. John 1:6-14

The Word and The Spirit

This entire selection in John is about the word of God. In the middle, a few verses speak about "the light" but then they switch back to the Word, stating that the Word was in the world, "He was in the world…" Only at the end does Jesus enter the scene, once the Word was made flesh. When it speaks of one who went to His own, this was again speaking of the Word. "It was in the world, and the world was made by it." From what we read before about Greek, I believe that this is how we may understand the verses, replacing "him" and "he" with "it." It was the Word of God that gave people the power to become the sons of God (see James 1:18). God's teaching, His doctrine, the gospel allowed them to do this. And so, if you follow this idea to the end of the selection, the Word was doing all of these things and finally it was made into flesh. God's teaching and His sayings were made into flesh, thus showing us the birth and early life of Christ. The Word being made flesh was not an instant occurrence, but it took place from Christ's birth and onward. This idea is reinforced when we understand the connection between the Word and the spirit. In John 6, Jesus spoke:

"It is the spirit that quickeneth; the flesh profiteth nothing: <u>the words that I speak unto you, they are spirit, and they are life</u>." John 6:63

The words of God and the words of Christ are spirit. They were God-breathed (2 Timothy 3:16). His Spirit wrote them (1 Peter 1:11). The point that we want to establish here in relation to John 1 is that the spirit and the Word are very closely connected. In fact, Jesus says that his words ARE spirit. If we can understand this connection, then the beginning of John will open up for us in an even greater way.

When reading through the beginning of the gospel of Luke, we read another version of the birth of Christ. In Luke, the angel Gabriel appears to Mary, telling her of God's favor upon her, revealing to her that she would have a son who would be called the son of God, and opening her eyes to the fact that he would fulfill the promises to David and would rule over the house of Israel. Imagine what it would be like to have an angel appear before you and reveal to you that you would be the parent of God's son! What a mind-blowing and intense experience this must have been for Mary. These are the words that we want to focus on:

"And the angel answered and said unto her, <u>The Holy Spirit shall come upon thee,</u> and the power of the Highest shall overshadow thee: <u>therefore also that holy thing which shall be born of thee shall be called the Son of God</u>." Luke 1:35

This verse is another blow to the Trinity. Notice that Mary would become pregnant from the HOLY SPIRIT. This is a very important point, because (in the language of the Trinity) if she became pregnant through the Holy Spirit, God the Holy Spirit would be Christ's Father, not God the Father. This makes the Trinity even more incomprehensible than it is originally. God the Father would no longer be God the Father (since He wouldn't be a Father). When we have a correct understanding of Scriptural Truth concerning God manifestation, we can understand it. God's power, which is a manifestation of the Holy Spirit, came upon Mary; her child would be called the Son of God. When we compare this verse to John 1:14, remembering that the spirit and the Word are intimately connected, possibly even synonymous at times, it is apparent that John is referring to the birth of Christ.

"And the Word was made flesh, and dwelt among us, (and we beheld his glory, the glory as of the only begotten of the Father,) full of grace and truth." John 1:14

The Word was made flesh, the Word that was God, and dwelt among us. We saw His glory, as of the only begotten of the Father. Understanding the connection between the Word and the spirit, that verse is essentially the same as the verse in Luke. John said that the Word would become flesh, Luke says that the Holy Spirit would come upon Mary and she would give birth to God's son!

From there, the verse then shows us the early childhood of Christ. Jesus being filled with the Word and becoming "the Word made flesh" was a process that was begun at his birth, and then continued on later. John gives us a time frame. He begins at his birth and then says "and we beheld his glory." All throughout that time, from his birth to when he began his ministry, Jesus was *becoming* "the Word...made flesh." This same idea is proclaimed in Luke:

"And Jesus <u>increased in wisdom</u> and stature, and in favour with God and man." Luke 2:52

As Jesus grew, he learned more of God's teaching, he learned more of the Word. He increased in wisdom. We can see the parallel between the two gospels, Luke and John. Luke tells us of the Holy Spirit coming upon Mary, her giving birth to the Son of God, and Jesus growing in wisdom and stature. John says all of these things very succinctly, with the statement "The Word was made flesh, and dwelt among us, (and we beheld his glory, the glory as of the only begotten of the Father,) full of grace and truth."

THE EXPLANATION

A quick summation of the introduction to John would go along these lines: The sayings of God, the Word, was present in the beginning; it was used to create the world and it was God. A man named John came to witness to the Word. Constantly this Word came to the people of God, through the prophets and the law, trying to get them to turn from their wicked deeds but they would not. To those who would believe, it gave them the power to become the children of God (James 1:18). Finally, the word of God became flesh and showed to us the kind of glory that only the Son of God could show.

DOES IT FIT JOHN'S THEMES?

In the beginning of this chapter, we looked at the themes of the gospel of John. We said that whatever explanation we come to about John 1, it must fit in with the purposes of the gospel, since these verses are the introduction, the place where John would want to preview the themes of his book. When we see John 1 as referring to the spoken word of God and of Christ's birth in verse 14, we see that our understanding fits in perfectly with the topics of the gospel. The two themes that we came upon were:

1. Jesus spoke God's words
2. Jesus is the son of God

From what we now understand of John 1, both of these topics are shown in verses 1-14 in a most graceful and glorious way. In the introduction of the gospel, Jesus is shown to be a speaker of God's words because he was all of those sayings, all of that teaching, put into flesh! Of course he would speak those words! In addition, this same introduction shows us that he is the son of God. It shows us the intimate relationship that Jesus had with his Father, and that the words of God were who he was, they were what were in his mind, and he was those words put into flesh. The Word was God, and he was the Word made flesh. He was begotten of the Word, which made the Word his Father. Thus, John ends the introduction with "We beheld his glory, the glory as of the only begotten of God." As the Word made flesh, Jesus was the SON OF GOD. He was his Father's Son. They thought the same, they had the same purpose.

And so, the proper understanding of John 1 teaches us about the Word of God, God's teachings and God's doctrine. It tells us that this Word was God and that it was used to create all things. It came into the world through preaching, and yet was rejected by the people. After sending the Word through multitudes of prophets, God put His spirit upon Mary and she gave birth to a son, a son who would become the Word made flesh. He would speak the words of his Father, he would think the thoughts of his Father, and he would follow his Father's will. All of this harmonizes with the teaching of John's gospel, and the teaching of Scripture.

"And the Word was Made Flesh"

A Summary

1. What are the two themes of John's gospel?

   - _____
   - _____

2. Fill in the blank: "In the beginning was the word, the word was with God, and the word was God. The same was in the beginning with God. _____ were made by him; without him was not any thing _____ that was _____."

3. What are two different definitions for the word "logos"? Give a verse for each.

   - _____
   - _____

4. God's sayings were used in creation. True/False

5. From our study, what is "the word"?

6. Explain how Greek can refer to an inanimate object or concept as "he" or "she."

7. Where does Jesus first appear in this passage?

   _____

8. Fill in the blank: Luke _____ gives a very interesting parallel to John 1:14.

9. How does our explanation fit in with the two themes of the gospel of John?

ANSWERS:

1. Jesus spoke the words of God; Jesus is God's son
2. All; made; made
3. Sayings or teachings (any of the verses from pgs. 138-139); purpose (Acts 10:29)
4. True
5. It is the things that God spoke, His words, His teaching
6. Greek gives all of their nouns either a masculine or a feminine gender. Thus, even if the noun is not alive, it still receives a gender.
7. Verse 14
8. 1:35
9. If Jesus is the Word made flesh, and the Word is God's sayings, it fits in perfectly with the idea of Jesus speaking God's words; also, if the Word is God, the Father, then Jesus is the Father put into flesh—this is basically the meaning of a son, the parents put into another person.

CHAPTER 7

THE FATHER AND THE CROSS

Throughout this book we have talked about God manifestation and how it has applied to others and to our hope. In this chapter, we will be examining the force that brings about God manifestation <u>in us</u>. In 2 Corinthians 5, Paul speaks about the atonement, or the death and resurrection of Christ.

"For <u>the love of Christ constraineth us</u>; because we thus judge, that if one died for all, then were all dead: and that he died for all, that <u>they which live should not henceforth live unto themselves, but unto him which died for them, and rose again</u>." 2 Corinthians 5:14-15

Essentially, what the apostle is telling us is that when we understand the atonement, when we realize that we were all dead and yet Christ rescued us from that death, then the understanding of God's great love in the atonement COMPELS us to change the way that we live. We are going to examine the atonement together. In this, we will see the motive behind Christ's death and resurrection, and the power of what happened that day outside Jerusalem. Seeing these things will lead us to follow in the footsteps of Christ and seek to reveal God through the way that we act.

"CHRISTIAN" ATONEMENT

As we begin, let us take a look at the way that most of the world understands the atonement. You've probably heard this idea before, maybe even believed it. I believed it for a good portion of my early years. The "Christian" view of the atonement is as follows:

As Jesus hung on the cross, the sins of humankind throughout the centuries began to appear on him. He could feel the wickedness, the pure evil that was crushing him under its weight. As the sin began to crawl upon His body, His Father looked at Him with fury in His eyes. "My son, you have despised my name, you have lied, you have cheated, you have murdered, you have hated my followers…" and He goes on, putting all of our sins upon His Son. He hates all of those things that He sees. He despises them, and turns His face away from Christ. Jesus cries "My God, my God, why have you forsaken me?" But the Father refuses to hear. His anger against humankind envelops and focuses directly upon His Son. He has forsaken Christ whom He loved. He has rejected Jesus. Christ's sacrifice satisfied His wrath and the reconciliation was complete. Sin brought death into the world and so someone had to die because of it. Jesus took the place of mankind and died instead of them. He satisfied God's anger.

This doctrine is horrendous. So many people in this world believe that Jesus died in our place, that all of our sin was placed upon Him. They say that we were in front of a firing squad, doomed to die because we were sinners, and then Jesus came to the One who was in charge of the killing, made a deal, and allowed us to go free while He died.

I have a video that I show when I give classes about this. The video is from a large local church and it is part of their beginning instruction, their essential doctrines that people need to know in order to become a Christian. In the video, the pastor talks about the atonement, about Christ's death, and says that one of the most important things we have to understand about it is that Jesus was our substitute. He took all of our sins, all of the evil that you have committed, and took it upon himself. This teaching is prevalent in the mainstream Christian community.

This picture of the atonement is incredibly sick and twisted. Everything is turned around. Whereas the Bible tells us that God gave Jesus out of love, mainstream Christians say that it is because God was wrathful and angry and needed to be pacified through someone dying. Whereas the Bible tells us that Jesus was sinless, this makes Him to be a gross sinner. Whereas the Bible tells us that we can be forgiven, this tells us that our sins were paid for. Whereas the Bible tells us that God and Christ were working together in His sacrifice, this tells us that they were divided against one another, with a wrathful Deity screaming against His son. If you don't believe that your church teaches this, go find out. Go ask your pastor about what happened on the cross, go ask them how God's wrath and justice entered into the crucifixion, and see what they say. This doctrine is extremely prevalent in modern Christianity. Sadly, it is a doctrine that completely and utterly maligns the righteous and beautiful Father, and His glorious son.

Jesus' sacrifice is made into a mockery, a gross picture of mythology.

Imagine how God feels about teachings like this. Writing that completely and utterly slanders His name, that takes the greatest gift of love that the world has ever seen, and disparages Him, saying that He needed to be appeased, that He was wrathful and so slew His own son in anger. Throwing the Trinity into all of that, He killed Himself in His anger. We cannot let ourselves believe blasphemy like this. Jesus was NOT our substitute. He did NOT die in our place. This idea of substitution is usually based in passages such as Isaiah 53:4, "surely he hath borne our griefs, and carried our sorrows" and 1 Peter 2:24, "Who his own self bare our sins in his own body on the tree." These passages are misunderstood and advanced to say that Jesus became personally responsible for all of the sins that we ever committed, and he took our place on the cross. This is not what happened, and this is not what the passages mean. The passages can be truly understood when we look at how Matthew quotes Isaiah 53 when Christ was healing people (Matthew 8:16-17). Jesus bore the infirmities of the sick by taking them away! He took those sicknesses from them and carried them away, but he never took them as his own! He didn't become sick after healing people! Jesus did not become personally responsible for our sins—he made it so that our sins could be taken away! He was not a substitute!

Instead, of showing God as an angry deity that needed to be satisfied, instead of painting the Father in an unfavorable light, Jesus' death was focused on bringing blessings and glory to God, to his Father. It was all about Him. Throughout this chapter, we will be examining the cross, or the atonement, and observing God's role in it. Is it true that God was angry at humanity? Did His righteousness demand that someone die for our sins? Did He kill His son in our place to placate His anger? Is it true that while Jesus was dying on the cross, His Father was shouting at him and despising him because our sins were making the Messiah a disgusting, sin-filled creature? As we study, we will see how the Truth of the atonement is completely and totally different than Christianity sees it, and instead of tearing down God's name, it actually lifts Him up. We will see that God, Yahweh, is actually an essential focus of Christ's sacrifice.

At the end of this chapter, it is my goal that you will come forth with a renewed and powerful understanding of the goodness of our God. Through this study, may you be able to better contemplate His love and seek to manifest Him by putting on His name through baptism. If you have already been baptized into Truth, may this chapter fan your the flame of zeal for God.

THE FATHER IS OUR SAVIOR

God had an amazing and irreplaceable role in the death and resurrection of Jesus. The whole focus of the atonement was on Him. Jesus died to bring honor and glory to his Father. Just as the purpose of God is to bring honor to Himself, the purpose of the atonement was to glorify Him as well. This can be seen just in the way that the title "Savior" is used about the Father. Most likely, when we think about the term "Savior," our minds almost immediately go to Jesus. "He is my Savior," we might think. This is completely true. Scripture is brimming with verses about Jesus being our Savior. But, while we are thinking on this, we may miss the fact that God, in fact, is also our Savior. Take a look at the following passages.

"And Mary said, My soul doth magnify the Lord, and my spirit hath rejoiced <u>in God my Savior.</u>"

Luke 1:46-47

"Paul, an apostle of Jesus Christ by the commandment of <u>God our Savior</u>, and Lord Jesus Christ, which is our hope." 1 Timothy 1:1

"To the only wise <u>God our Savior</u>, be glory and majesty, dominion and power, both now and ever. Amen." Jude 1:25

This is not just a New Testament concept, but over and over in the Old Testament, God is called a "Savior."

"Tell ye, and bring them near; yea, let them take counsel together: who hath declared this from ancient time? who hath told it from that time? have not I the LORD? and there is no God else beside me; <u>a just God and a Savior</u>; there is none beside me." Isaiah 45:21

The most emphatic of all these passages is in Isaiah 43. In it, we are told that Yahweh is the ONLY Savior.

"I, even I, am the LORD; and <u>beside me there is no savior</u>." Isaiah 43:11

The emphasis here is powerful. There is NO savior but God. This is not to say that Jesus is not our savior, but rather that Jesus was our savior because God was working through him (Acts 2:22). Picture it this way: we were drowning in the water, and a man threw us a life preserver. Who then saved us, the life preserver or the man who threw it? Both of them did. Without the preserver, the man would have needed to find another way to save us. Without the man, the preserver would have never been thrown. Jesus was and is much more than a life preserver, so please pardon the analogy. However, when looking at the framework on this situation, the atonement is a similar picture. God was working through Jesus to save us. God is the Savior, and because God was working through Christ, Jesus is also the Savior. In no way is this meant to minimize the pain and agony that Jesus went through. It is said to help us focus on God's role in the atonement, and to see that the purpose of the atonement was to glorify Him!

This presents us with an extremely important point— the atonement was a passionate gift of love and obedience by our Lord Jesus. At the same time, it was also a painful, powerful, and immense gift from our Father. God is our SAVIOR and besides Him there is NO OTHER SAVIOR. Jesus is our Savior because God was saving THROUGH him. He was using Jesus to save us. BY NO MEANS was the atonement a face off between the son and the Father. By no means was the atonement a time in which God forsook His beloved son and unleashed His anger upon Christ. These blasphemous thoughts have no place in the minds and hearts of those who seek to know the true God and Savior of Israel.

TEAMWORK

Often, as we mentioned, Jesus is seen as our savior, the one who died for us, the one who gave up his life and who gave up on every single time that he desired to sin. This is entirely true—he is our Savior, and the Savior of the world. Yet in the actual act of SAVING us, Jesus was NOT alone. We know that all of the time that Christ hung on the cross, God was there with him.

To better understand this, let us take a look at a Biblical echo. Isaac was the son of Abraham, who was mentioned earlier in chapter 3. At one time (Genesis 22), God called upon

Abraham to sacrifice his son Isaac (thankfully, it all ended up fine, Isaac did not actually have to die, but God wanted to see how dedicated Abraham truly was to Him). This sacrifice of Isaac provides an excellent parallel to the sacrifice of Christ. Below are a few examples of the similarities in the situations:

Abraham and Isaac	God and Jesus
Isaac was a promised son (Genesis 18:10; 21:1-3)	Jesus was a promised son (Luke 1:30-33)
Isaac was referred to as the only son (Genesis 22:2)	Jesus was referred to as the only son (John 3:16)
Abraham knew that Isaac would be resurrected (Genesis 22:5; Hebrews 11:19)	God knew that Jesus would be resurrected (Psalm 16:10)
Isaac carried the wood for the sacrifice (Genesis 22:6)	Jesus carried the cross (John 19:17)
Abraham was going to give up his son (Genesis 22:10)	God gave up His son (John 3:16)

Isaac showed us a type of what was to come in the Lord Jesus. Now, ask yourself this question: did Abraham ever leave Isaac while he was on the altar? Did Abraham strap Isaac to the altar, then tell him to stay there while he went off some distance and shot him with an arrow, or was Abraham there the entire time? Throughout this scene, Abraham NEVER left Isaac's side. He was there giving Isaac encouragement, support, and strength. So it was with God. When Christ was on the cross, God was there with him, helping him to get through it, helping him to remember the joy that was set before him. Second Corinthians tells us this:

"And all things are of God, who hath reconciled us to himself by Jesus Christ, and hath given to us the ministry of reconciliation; to wit, <u>that God was in Christ</u>, reconciling the world unto himself, not imputing their trespasses unto them; and hath committed unto us the word of reconciliation."
2 Corinthians 5:18-19

Not only was God there with Jesus, but He was IN Jesus, giving him strength. Jesus tells us similar words when speaking to his disciples. They would all leave him that night, but his Father would NEVER LEAVE HIS SIDE.

"Behold, the hour cometh, yea, is now come, that ye shall be scattered, every man to his own, and shall leave me alone: and yet <u>I am not alone, because the Father is with me</u>." John 16:32

While Jesus was suffering, God was there suffering with him. God was in Christ, giving Christ that strength, leading him to his work, and bringing the world back into grace with Him. God was there, working with Jesus, never forsaking him and never leaving him. By no means did the atonement have to do with a God who was angry, punishing His son for the sins of all humanity. Never! The atonement, the reconciliation, was an act of God working together with Jesus; it was an act of Jesus humbly submitting to the leadership of Almighty God, and working together with that God to give fallen humanity a way to come back to grace.

After hearing this, that God was always with Christ all throughout his death, it may seem odd to us that Jesus said "My God, My God, why hast thou forsaken me?" (Matthew 27:46). Here, Jesus is actually quoting Psalm 22:1, which says the exact same thing. In fact, if you compare the verses of Psalm 22 to the verses of Christ's crucifixion in Matthew, you will find many similarities. This is a study that I highly recommend. If you have not already done it, you will benefit greatly from comparing the two chapters. The resurrection is even implicitly hidden within Psalm 22:22, which speaks of the one who is "crushed," living again to declare God's name. Christ was not forsaken by God! Instead, he was seeking to bring the Jews who were at the cross, who would have known the Psalms, back to Psalm 22. He wanted them to realize that they were fulfilling that prophecy, that God KNEW what they were going to do to His son, and that possibly this would cause them to repent and be forgiven! Even at the very last moment of his life while he was being tortured, Jesus was thinking of others and their hope. NEVER was Jesus forsaken by God. But, as we are told, God was there with Christ, helping him to get through this trial.

The Bible gives us the picture of a God who is a Savior. It does not show us a terribly angry God, who lusts after blood and is only appeased once something has died for sin. No! It shows us a God who was working to save, it shows us a God who is the SAVIOR of mankind!

HEREIN IS LOVE

Scripture shows a God who saw that mankind was destined to die, and created a plan to save them. It shows us that the atonement was an act of love. It was not a violent death to appease God's wrath. Instead, it was a loving way in which God could rescue fallen man. The atonement was a gift from our Father. It is His expression of love and care for us. Take a look at these passages and notice the emotion that is behind them. The first is a very familiar verse to all of us:

"For God so loved the world, that he gave his only begotten Son, that whosoever believeth in him should not perish, but have everlasting life." John 3:16

What emotion comes forth here? LOVE. Our Lord looked upon this fallen creation and did not want it to always be this way. He did not want society to be run by wickedness, He did not want His creation to run around mindlessly serving their flesh, beating and killing anything that got in their way. In His love, He sent Jesus to show us who He truly is, to manifest Him, and to bid us to follow in his steps in a full-life sacrifice. The following references are more Scriptural evidence that this was the case:

"In this was manifested the love of God toward us, because that God sent his only begotten Son into the world, that we might live through him. Herein is love, not that we loved God, but that he loved us, and sent his Son to be the propitiation for our sins." 1 John 4:9-10

What is the emotion shown here? Again, it is love!

"For when we were yet without strength, in due time Christ died for the ungodly. For scarcely for a righteous man will one die: yet peradventure for a good man some would even dare to die. But God commendeth his love toward us, in that, while we were yet sinners, Christ died for us." Romans 5:6-8

Once more, God's love is shown to us. This passage is even more passionate than the others. Rather than just speaking about God's love, this passage speaks of the MAGNITUDE, the GREATNESS of His love. We are told: It is rare to find someone who would be willing to die for a righteous person, someone who would be willing to give up their life for someone who is "good." But, try looking for someone who would give up their life for a SINNER! It is basically impossible, no one would want to give up their life for someone who lives a life of sin. But God showed His LOVE for us, because while we were still sinners, while we were still loving our sin and living in it, God sent His son to die for us, to give us an example of faith, and to show us that we need to CRUCIFY our sins and live a new life.

FORGIVEN

All throughout the atonement, God's goodness is shown to us. We see that He is our Savior; we see that He was working with Christ, giving him support and strength; and we see that the atonement was a gift of His love. God's goodness and lovingkindness come out of the atonement in another way still. In the false view of the atonement, Jesus pays for our sins with His blood. However, Scripture teaches us that God FORGIVES our sins, rather than being paid for them. Think about this as an example—

Imagine that you owe the government $500,000,000,000 (500 billion dollars). That's a lot of money. Because it is such a huge sum, and you will never make that much money in your life, you decide to forget about it and hope that the government will as well. One day, as you are eating dinner with your family, you hear the doorbell ring. Since you're a friendly person, you get up and answer the door. The president, with his entourage, is standing before you. You have not paid your debt. As he stands in front of you, the president looks in your eyes and says, "You owe me a large chunk of money. Since you haven't paid it back yet, I am going to assume that you can't pay. So, I'm going to take everything that you own and throw you in jail. I am going to take your wife and your children. You will all work until you pay me back." This is the worst thing that could happen to you. Immediately, you fall down on your knees and beg him, "Please Mr. President! I will repay the debt, give me a chance!" This does not faze him. His guards begin to step forward, unhooking their handcuffs from their belts. However, right as his guards are about to handcuff you, one of his children jumps in front of him and says, "Dad, I don't want this person to suffer like this. I've saved up over the years and I'll pay the $500,000,000,000 back." They pull out their checkbook and immediately write a check to the president and you are free!

Think about this story for a few seconds, and then answer these questions:

1. *Does your freedom have anything to do with the president's goodness?*
2. *Was your debt forgiven or paid for?*
3. *Is the president a merciful man?*

This is a major problem when we come to the idea of substitution. The answers to these questions, at best, are 1) not really; 2) paid for; 3) maybe sometimes, but not in this situation. Many Christians are taught that this is what happened at the atonement. The focus is completely on Jesus, who stood before God's wrath and pacified it so that we would not die; Jesus paid our debt with his blood and satisfied God's anger. But, as we read, the atonement was a gift of love! It was an act in which the God of the universe looked on us, who were nasty sinners, and gave us a means to be saved. It was done out of compassion. It wasn't done out of a desire to be repaid! We see this illustrated in the fact that our sins were NOT PAID FOR, but instead they were forgiven. Take

a look at Matthew 18, the BIBLICAL version of the story
that you just read.

> Therefore is the kingdom of heaven likened unto a
> certain king, which would take account of his
> servants. And when he had begun to reckon, one was
> brought unto him, which owed him ten thousand
> talents. But forasmuch as he had not to pay, his lord
> commanded him to be sold, and his wife, and
> children, and all that he had, and payment to be
> made. The servant therefore fell down, and
> worshipped him, saying, Lord, have patience with me,
> and I will pay thee all. <u>Then the lord of that servant
> was moved with compassion, and loosed him, and
> forgave him the debt.</u> Matthew 18:23-27

The ending of this story of is very different than the ending
that I had told to you. The focus and hero of this story is the
Lord! He is the one that saved the debtor! It is the same with
our situation. BECAUSE OF THE LOVE AND
COMPASSION of the Father, our debt is FORGIVEN.
There is no payment. All that you owed was never repaid!
God said "I will wipe it clean and you will not have to think
about it." Because of His great goodness, because of His
mercy, because of His compassion, He does not receive
payment. Think about the difference there, and see how
much better this reflects upon the Father. Instead of turning
Him into a greedy king, He is a king who chooses to
FORGIVE what you have done. He chooses to wash it away.
We worship a truly wonderful God. The following verses will
reaffirm this same idea, that God has FORGIVEN us and has
NOT been given a payment for our debts.

"<u>And forgive us our sins</u>; for we also forgive every one that is indebted to us. And lead us not into temptation; but deliver us from evil." Luke 11:4

"And be ye kind one to another, tenderhearted, forgiving one another, even as God for Christ's sake <u>hath forgiven you</u>." Ephesians 4:32

"If we confess our sins, he is faithful and just <u>to forgive us our sins</u>." 1 John 1:9

God **FORGIVES** our sins. There is no payment of debt involved.

It may be confusing to say that Jesus didn't pay for our sins, because Scripture mentions things like Jesus being a ransom and us being bought with a price. I want to mention that it is perfectly and wonderfully Scriptural for us to use the phrases "you were bought with a price" and Jesus came as a "ransom for many" (1 Corinthians 6:20 and Matthew 20:28). Both of these phrases **DO** give an idea of payment. The important thing for us to notice here is the **OBJECT** that has been bought or paid for. Was it a debt for our sins? Not at all! Instead, "**YOU** were bought with a price" and Jesus was a "ransom for **MANY**." Many people can get confused from these verses and think that they are teaching that Jesus **DID** pay for our sins. Rather, they are teaching that Jesus' death did have a payment aspect to it, but the payment was for us, to free us from being the servants of sin, it was not for our sins themselves. Sins are forgiven by God because of His compassion.

From our studies, we can see that the atonement places the focus upon the Father. It shows us that He is our

Savior, that He and Christ were working together on the cross, that the motivation for the atonement was LOVE, and that He did not receive a payment but rather chose to forgive sins.

TO DECLARE HIS RIGHTEOUSNESS

Since we can understand that God forgives our sins, doesn't receive a payment for them, and orchestrated the atonement as an act of love, these questions may come to our minds: "Why then did Jesus have to die?" and "Why did He have to suffer so much?" Again, the scriptural answer focuses our thoughts toward the Father:

> Being justified freely by his grace through the redemption that is in Christ Jesus: whom God hath set forth to be a propitiation through faith in his blood, <u>to declare his righteousness</u> for the remission of sins that are past, through the forbearance of God; <u>to declare, I say, at this time his righteousness</u>: that he might be just, and the justifier of him which believeth in Jesus. Romans 3:24-26

Jesus died to show God's righteousness. In short, Jesus was a man just like us, with a fleshly nature. He got on the cross and crucified that nature, showing to the entire world for centuries to come that his FLESH deserved to die, even though he never committed sin. He showed the God was right in sending him to the cross—in condemning his flesh. Through that, he declared God's righteousness. Let's take a look at it a bit more in-depth.

A WAR WITH SIN

As we look at Christ's actual death on the cross, there are two things that we have to understand:

1. God is in a war with the flesh
2. Jesus had human nature with all of its inclinations

The first point is something that all of us know. God hates sin, He hates the sin which begins in our flesh. He is at war with sin. It is something that He despises. Since the fall of Adam and Eve, God has been fighting against it.

"And I will put enmity between thee and the woman, and between thy seed and her seed, it shall bruise thy head, and thou shalt bruise his heel." Genesis 3:15

The seed of the woman, the followers of God, would always be at enmity with the seed of the serpent, those who loved wickedness. They would constantly be at war. We know that God hates the evil that comes from our hearts. Constantly, Scripture is speaking to us of things that are an abomination to God. These are all things that proceed from our FLESH.

"For the wicked boasteth of his heart's desire, and blesseth the covetous, whom the LORD abhorreth." Psalm 10:3

"The LORD trieth the righteous: but the wicked and him that loveth violence his soul hateth." Psalm 11:5

"For the froward is abomination to the LORD: but his secret is with the righteous." Proverbs 3:32

"The way of the wicked is an abomination unto the LORD: but he loveth him that followeth after righteousness." Proverbs 15:9

God hates the wicked, the perverse, the covetous. He hates those who take pleasure in sin, those who revel in the ways of the world. He is in a war with this type of behavior, which all stems from the flesh. The flesh is the root of sin. To clarify, God doesn't hate the FLESH itself, but He despises the SIN that comes from it. Unfortunately, our flesh cannot stand against its own temptations. God is warring against those temptations.

"Because the carnal mind is enmity against God: for it is not subject to the law of God, neither indeed can be." Romans 8:7

It is the carnal mind that brings about the terrible, evil thoughts that we have. This mind is enmity against God. It cannot be subject to His law, and it cannot honor Him. It says that its ways are right, even though they are directly opposed to God's, and it calls God's ways wrong. When we want to understand how Jesus' death declared God's righteousness, we need to recognize that God is in a war with sin.

HUMAN NATURE

The second point that is essential to our understanding of the atonement is that Jesus possessed a human nature which was inclined to sin. His nature was just like ours—it was the root of sin. It would try to get Christ to follow different temptations, but he never gave in. Jesus was tempted, but he never sinned! This is a beautiful thing for us to recognize because it makes his humanity and sacrifice so much more real. There were points in Jesus' life, like the temptations in the wilderness, where part of him was tempted to do what was wrong. AND YET HE NEVER GAVE IN TO IT AT ALL. Take a look at Hebrews 4.

"For we have not an high priest which cannot be touched with the feeling of our infirmities; but was in all points tempted like as we are, yet without sin." Hebrews 4:15

Jesus was tempted, but he always turned to God. He looked to his Father for strength, and never actually sinned.

DESTROYING THE DEVIL

Jesus was tempted to do wrong, but never did. In fact, he was even tempted to not go to the cross. He didn't want to, but he did anyway, showing his loving obedience (Matthew 26:39). Every day of his life, he put that temptation to death, put his flesh to death by resisting its urges. He never once gave in. And finally, one day, he literally did kill those urges. That day was the day of his death on the cross.

"Forasmuch then as the children are partakers of flesh and blood, he also himself likewise took part of the same; that through death he might destroy him that has the power of death, that is, the devil." Hebrews 2:14

Notice the quadruple emphasis in this verse. HE, ALSO, HIMSELF, LIKEWISE. The writer is trying to put it into our minds that Jesus most definitely was flesh, just like us. Just as we, the children, are flesh and blood, Jesus was flesh and blood as well. He took part in this nature, so that he could destroy the devil. Jesus had a fleshly nature so that all throughout his life he could deny that flesh and finally put it

173

to death on the cross. This is what his death was about. The devil referred to here isn't some type of supernatural evil being, but it was his flesh, the stem of temptation. Jesus hung up on that cross to show generations to come that our flesh—not sin itself, but the root of sin—deserved to be crucified. He was killed to show that despite the fact that He had NEVER sinned, the FLESH still deserved to die. Its tendencies were ALWAYS warring against the mind of God, as we said. He shouted out God's righteousness while he was on that cross because he showed the world that even though he was blameless, this was what should happen to flesh. It should be destroyed, its desires should be put away. This is reinforced by Romans 8:3.

"For what the law could not do, in that it was weak through the flesh, God sending his own Son in the likeness of sinful flesh, and for sin, <u>condemned sin in the flesh</u>." Romans 8:3

It is almost the exact same thing said as Hebrews 2:14. By coming in the likeness of sinful flesh, by having our nature, Jesus condemned sin in the flesh! Jesus condemned our flesh, the root of sin. He condemned the devil. He killed it by fighting against it all of his life and finally crucifying it. Flesh was destroyed. God was victorious, Jesus had followed Him in perfect obedience.

FOLLOWING HIS STEPS

As we look at this new picture of the atonement, we see our God in the pure light of Scripture. Over and over we can see the compassion, the love, and the mercy of the Father. We see a VERY different picture of the atonement than what modern Christianity shows us. Instead of seeing an angry deity who needs to be appeased by the blood of His son, we see a God who loved us and wanted to rescue us for the glory of His name. The Truth gives us a real picture of the true God—a picture that we can trust.

Jesus was not our substitute. He was our representative. He hung on the cross to declare God's righteousness. However, this means nothing to us unless we follow him; Jesus' death calls us to take up our cross and follow him! If he were our substitute, we would be free to do whatever we want. He would have died instead of us, and we would not have to die. We could live in whatever way we chose.

Instead, Scripture tells us that the atonement is an example to us. We need to look at Jesus hanging on the cross and say "I need to do that. I need to declare God's righteousness just as he did." We need to be willing to give up ourselves to God, we need to crucify our flesh and it's desires, we need to place our feet in Jesus' footsteps, and follow him.

"For even hereunto were ye called: because Christ also suffered for us, leaving us an example, that <u>ye should follow his steps</u>." 1 Peter 2:21

He was our example. We need to follow him.

"And he said to them all, If any man will come after me, let him deny himself, <u>and take up his cross daily</u>, and follow me." Luke 9:23

Each day we need to crucify our flesh. Each day we need to focus our lives on manifesting God, on declaring His righteousness. The love of Christ constrains us to live in a new way!

"For whosoever will save his life shall lose it; but <u>whosoever shall lose his life for my sake</u> and the gospel's, the same shall save it." Mark 8:35

And so WE must give up our lives.

BURIED BY BAPTISM

The Father has set out a way for us to do this. We don't literally have to hang, bleed, and die on a cross as Christ did. God, in His mercy, has given us baptism as a way to follow Jesus. Through baptism, we can bury our "old man" and be born again as a "new man" when we come up out of the water.

"Therefore <u>we are buried with him by baptism into death</u>: that like as Christ was raised up from the dead by the glory of the Father, even so we also should walk in newness of life." Romans 6:4

When we are baptized, we are dying with Jesus. Just as he was resurrected to new life, to immortality, when we are raised up out of the water, we too need to live a new life. We are now called to manifest God. We are called to show God's characteristics just as Christ did and now does. Skipping up to verses 6-7, Paul emphasizes this point. Our body of sin is destroyed, so that we no longer live to sin.

"Knowing this, that our old man is crucified with him, that the body of sin might be destroyed, <u>that henceforth we should not serve sin</u>. For he that is dead is freed from sin." Romans 6:6-7

When we die with Jesus, we recognize that our lives are all about God. We recognize that he, being righteous and all powerful, deserves all of our praise and love. And so all of the things that once mattered to us, they are counted as NOTHING. We recognize that our treasure is spiritual, that it is held in the relationship that we have with God and with Christ.

> But what things were gain to me, those I counted loss for Christ. Yea doubtless, and I count all things but loss for the excellency of the knowledge of Christ Jesus my Lord: for whom I have suffered the loss of all things, and do count them but dung, that I may win Christ. Philippians 3:7-8

The cross and a proper understanding of the atonement leads us to God manifestation. It leads us to following the footsteps of Jesus. We need to be thinking about Christ, we need to "look unto Jesus, the author and finisher of our faith." Regardless of whether or not we are baptized, looking upon the cross, realizing the love and power behind Christ's sacrifice MUST compel us to action.

The Father deserves all of the praise that this world can offer to Him. He is the Savior. He sent Jesus out of love. He offers forgiveness for sins. He is righteous! We see all of these different principles set out to us when we look upon Christ's sacrifice, when we look upon the atonement. In addition, we also see that Jesus was our representative, not our substitute. His dedication to the Father is an example to all of us. He loved God in a living and passionate way. Let us follow in his footsteps and take up our cross daily.

THE FATHER AND THE CROSS

A Summary

1. How do you think God feels about the false view of the atonement promoted by much of Christianity?

2. The Father is our Savior. Provide three verses that prove this point.

   _____   _____

   _____

3. God forsook Jesus on the Cross. True/False

4. Multiple Choice:
   What was God's emotion behind the atonement:
   a. God doesn't have emotions
   b. Joy
   c. Anger
   d. Hatred
   e. Love

5. Did God forgive our sins or were they paid for? Prove with two verses.

6. How did Jesus' death show God's righteousness?

7. Fill in the blank: We can follow Jesus to the cross by
   _____. After this, we must strive to live a new life
   following, or manifesting _____ in everything we do.

ANSWERS:

1. He hates it.
2. Any of the verses from pgs. 159-160
3. False
4. e.
5. He forgave our sins. Any of the verses on pgs. 168-169
6. He was obedient to God even when he had never sinned and didn't deserve to die. He crucified his flesh, the root of sin.
7. Baptism; God

CHAPTER 8

CONCLUSION

Throughout this book we have turned through the pages of Scripture and seen the Truth that God has revealed in His Word. We have seen the REVEALED mystery. The type of attitude that seeks to understand, that prays for open eyes, is the type of attitude that pleases the Father. It is the seeking attitude of Daniel and the prayerful attitude of Nehemiah that God seeks to create in His servants. We cannot just say "it is a mystery" and not look any further into the Word of Truth. When we do look further, our understanding of God and His plan shines forth vividly.

And now we see that this idea of God manifestation is much larger than it may have originally seemed. Instead of just relating to Jesus Christ, it actually reaches out to us, to our friends, to our children, and our hope in this world. From God manifestation, we see what the Bible teaches about the relationship between Jesus and God. Rather than stating that the son and Father are one essence and that we will be with them forever, we have a much more definite understanding of God and of the hope we can have. We can say with confidence that Jesus was a perfect representative of God, one who showed the character of God wherever he went. Now, after his obedience, he possesses the actual name of God. It is his name. By the grace of the Father, it can be our name someday. We can be immortal, showing forth God's character to all. We can be engaged to Jesus. We can say with firmness that one day we can be made one with him in a beautiful marriage. Truly, God has offered us a great blessing.

This hope is a gift from God. Before it can be given, we must learn to follow in the footsteps of Jesus, we must learn to manifest God TODAY. The sacrifice of Christ shows us the type of love and dedication we must have for the Father. We see Jesus on the cross, declaring God to be righteous, and we realize that we must take up our cross as well, that we must then manifest the characteristics of the Father in the things that we do. The atonement shows us who our God really is, and compels us to follow in the steps of Christ. God is our Savior, and through His MERCY and LOVE we can be FORGIVEN. The blasphemous falsities of mainstream Christianity are nowhere to be found in the pages of the Bible.

God will fulfill His purpose with this earth. When His followers are united with His son, when their vile bodies are changed to be like Christ's glorious body, when their minds are changed to think godly things, then God's character will be shown through us, His representatives. Eventually, when sin is destroyed, the only thing left in the world will be a creation which sings the praises of its Creator. This is the picture that I want to leave with you. May you take these words into your heart and may it motivate you to keep seeking God, to keep studying His word, and to strive with all of your being to manifest Him. As He has promised: "All the earth shall be filled with the glory of the LORD"; may you and I both be at that marriage, when His glory begins to fill the globe, and may we be united to the Lord Jesus, showing forth the character of the Father.

"Blessed be the LORD God, the God of Israel, who only doeth wondrous things. And blessed be his glorious name for ever: and <u>let the whole earth be filled with his glory</u>; Amen, and Amen." Psalm 72:18-19

ACKNOWLEDGEMENTS

Thanks be to God for the strength, the ability, and the time to put this book together. All of the glory goes to Him.

This book is dedicated to the Simi Hills Christadelphian Youth Circle. To see so many of you grow in your love of Scripture and our Father has been a source of strength for me. I love you all so much, and cannot wait to share the Kingdom together. Keep loving the Truth. Never let it go. Let it transform you into a true disciple.

Many people helped out in working on this book. I specifically want to thank Ruth, my fiancee, for her support and encouragement. It has been such a joy to be able to talk to you about my studies, to be able to pray with you about this endeavor, and to be able to share ideas together. Your flexibility and supportive words have been a treasure; and your proofreading was invaluable. I love you.

Thanks to the three brethren who were willing to read this work and check my studies: Brother Bob Lloyd, Brother John McConville, and Brother Tom Graham. Your examples in the Truth have been inspirational to me.

Thanks also to Brother Ken Sommerville for being the one who read through my initial draft and helped me to move in the right direction. Thank you for your love, support, and example.

Finally, thanks to the Simi Hills Ecclesia. This ecclesia has been a source of strength and love for me as I have grown up. I love each of you with all of my heart. Thank you for helping me to grow in the Truth and grow in love for our Father.

SOURCES

An Etymological Essay on the Grammatical Sense in the Greek of the Sacred Texts Regarding the Last Supper. John Joseph Dillon. 1836. Public Domain.

The Divine Trinity. Joseph Pohle. 1911. Public Domain.

A Greek and English Lexicon to the New Testament. John Parkhurst. 1813. Public Domain.

A Greek Grammar for Schools and Colleges. Herbert Weir Smyth. 1916. Public Domain.

The Holy Bible, English Standard Version, copyright 2001 by Crossway Bibles, a publishing ministry of Good News Publishers. Used by permission. All rights reserved.

The Holy Bible, King James Version. 1611. Public Domain.

The Mighty Mystery. George W. Mylne. 1866. Public Domain.

Strong's Exhaustive Concordance of the Bible. James Strong. 1890. Hendrickson.

Works of the Late Reverend John Paul. John Paul and Stewart Bates. 1855. Public Domain.

Printed in Great Britain
by Amazon.co.uk, Ltd.,
Marston Gate.